Lasting Legacy:

making a difference with my life

Bible Study That Builds Christian Community

SERENDIPITY
H O U S E

LIFE
CONNECTIONS

ISBN: 1-5749-4070-8
Item 001208802

Unless otherwise indicated, all Scripture quotations are from the Holy Bible,
New International Version, copyright © 1973, 1978, 1984
by International Bible Society. Used by permission.

To order additional copies of this resource:
ORDER ONLINE at *www.serendipityhouse.com*;
VISIT the LifeWay Christian Store serving you;
WRITE Serendipity House
One LifeWay Plaza
Nashville, TN 37234-0175
FAX 615-277-8181

1-800-525-9563
www.SerendipityHouse.com

Printed in the United States of America

Contents

Core Values

Community: The purpose of this curriculum is to build community within the body of believers around Jesus Christ.

Group Process: To build community, the curriculum must be designed to take a group through a step-by-step process of sharing your story with one another.

Interactive Bible Study: To share your "story," the approach to Scripture in the curriculum needs to be open-ended and right-brained—to "level the playing field" and encourage everyone to share.

Developmental Stages: To provide a healthy program in the life cycle of a group, the curriculum needs to offer courses on three levels of commitment:

(1) Beginner Level—low-level entry, high structure, to level the playing field;

(2) Growth Level—deeper Bible study, flexible structure, to encourage group accountability;

(3) Discipleship Level—in-depth Bible study, open structure, to move the group into high gear.

Target Audiences: To build community throughout the culture of the church, the curriculum needs to be flexible, adaptable, and transferable into the structure of the average church.

Mission: To expand the kingdom of God one person at a time by filling the "empty chair." (We add an extra chair to each group session to remind us of our mission.)

Group Covenant

It is important that your group covenant together, agreeing to live out important group values. Once these values are agreed upon, your group will be on its way to experiencing Christian community. It's very important that your group discuss these values—preferably as you begin this study. The first session would be most appropriate. (Check the rules to which each member of your group agrees.)

- [ ] **Priority:** While you are in this course of study, you give the group meetings priority.
- [ ] **Participation:** Everyone is encouraged to participate and no one dominates.
- [ ] **Respect:** Everyone is given the right to his or her own opinion, and all questions are encouraged and respected.
- [ ] **Confidentiality:** Anything that is said in the meeting is never repeated outside the meeting.
- [ ] **Life Change:** We will regularly assess our own life-change goals and encourage one another in our pursuit of Christlikeness.
- [ ] **Empty Chair:** The group stays open to reaching new people at every meeting.
- [ ] **Care and Support:** Permission is given to call upon each other at any time, especially in times of crisis. The group will provide care for every member.
- [ ] **Accountability:** We agree to let the members of the group hold us accountable to the commitments we make in whatever loving ways we decide upon.
- [ ] **Mission:** We will do everything in our power to start a new group.
- [ ] **Ministry:** The group will encourage one another to volunteer and serve in a ministry and to support missions by giving financially and/or personally serving.

notes

connect
grow
serve

1

Sharing My Spiritual Story

Prepare for the Session

	READINGS	REFLECTIVE QUESTIONS
Monday	Galatians 1:11–12	Reflect on the time when you first heard the good news about Jesus and what He could do for you.
Tuesday	Galatians 1:13–14	What was your life like before knowing Christ?
Wednesday	Galatians 1:15–17	How did your life change after you chose to become a Christian?
Thursday	Galatians 1:18–20	Who helped you learn more and directed you to become more like Christ when you were a new believer?
Friday	Galatians 1:21–22	Who do you know who needs Jesus?
Saturday	Galatians 1:23	What do people say about your values, your character, and your actions?
Sunday	Galatians 1:24	Take time to praise God for the grace you have received.

BIBLE STUDY
- to learn how Paul told other people his story of how he became a Christian
- to understand the importance of sharing our own spiritual stories
- to look at some elements to include when we share our spiritual stories

LIFE CHANGE
- to listen to the spiritual stories of two mature Christians this week
- to write out in 250 words or less our spiritual stories
- to learn to share our spiritual stories naturally and from memory by telling them to at least one other person this week

Icebreaker

10-15 minutes

Where I'm Coming From. Mark an "X" on the following continuums to let us know "where you're coming from":

I was raised mostly in:

a small town · a big city

all over

The atmosphere of my childhood home was for the most part:

tense and hostile · · · · · · · · · · | · · · · · · · · · · · · peaceful and loving

In terms of what our family had, I was:

deprived · · · · · · · · · *Pat middle – Catholic* · · · · · *Ann* privileged

My religious training was:

nonexistent · *Pat's almost* stifling

almost

I learned to see the world mostly as:

dangerous · · · · · · · · · · · *Ann midway* · · · · · · · · · · *Pat* safe

8

Information to Remember: In the spaces provided, take note of information you will need as part of this group in the weeks to come. This week answer these questions during or after the session.

PEOPLE: A person I didn't know before attending this class is:

_____(first name)_____(last name)

I will recognize this person in the future because _____

_____(something unique about him or her).

EVENTS: An event that is coming up that I want to make sure I am part of is _____. It will be _____ (time) on _____ (date) at _____ (location).

And if I have time, I would also like to be part of _____. It will be _____ (time) on _____ (date) at _____ (location).

Bible Study

30-45 minutes

The Scripture for this week:

LEARNING FROM THE BIBLE

GALATIANS 1:11–24

[11] I want you to know, brothers, that the gospel I preached is not something that man made up. [12] I did not receive it from any man, nor was I taught it; rather, I received it by revelation from Jesus Christ.

[13] For you have heard of my previous way of life in Judaism, how intensely I persecuted the church of God and tried to destroy it. [14] I was advancing in Judaism beyond many Jews of my own age and was extremely zealous for the traditions of my fathers. [15] But when God, who set me apart from birth and called me by his grace, was pleased [16] to reveal his Son in me so that I might preach him among the Gentiles, I did not consult any man, [17] nor did I go up to Jerusalem to see those who were apostles before I was, but I went immediately into Arabia and later returned to Damascus.

[18] Then after three years, I went up to Jerusalem to get acquainted with Peter and stayed with him fifteen days. [19] I saw none of the other apostles—only James, the Lord's brother. [20] I assure you before God that what I am writing you is no lie. [21] Later I went to Syria and Cilicia.

²²I was personally unknown to the churches of Judea that are in Christ. ²³They only heard the report: "The man who formerly persecuted us is now preaching the faith he once tried to destroy." ²⁴And they praised God because of me.

...about today's session

1. According to this presentation, what is a gift only you can give?

2. What kind of feedback do we need to get from others?

Identifying with the Story

1. If you could point to one area of activity where, as a teenager, you were advancing beyond many of your own age, what area would it be?

   - ☐ sports
   - ☐ music
   - ☐ street smarts
   - ☐ maturity
   - ☐ verbal ability
   - ☐ social confidence
   - ☐ mechanical ability
   - ☐ knowledge of my hobby area
   - ☐ ability to get myself out of trouble
   - ☐ academics
   - ☐ knowledge of the Bible
   - ☐ business acumen
   - ☐ dramatic ability
   - ☐ sophistication
   - ☐ other:_____

2. What do you remember doing as a youth that you are now ashamed of?

- ☐ lying to my parents
- ☐ teasing a kid in the neighborhood or at school
- ☐ being a racist
- ☐ teasing or hurting a sibling
- ☒ partying too much
- ☐ making fun of the Christian kids
- ☐ shoplifting
- ☐ other:_____

3. How would you describe your attitude toward God when you were a teen? *nonexistent*

Pat distant

today's session

What is God teaching you from this story?

1. What things happened in Paul's life that could have made him hesitant to share his spiritual story with others?

Was intolerant, persecuted Christians

2. What two reasons did Paul have for sharing his story with the Galatians?

Salvation story - met Jesus on Damascus Rd

_____

3. What three elements does the leader encourage you to include when you tell your spiritual story?

1. *tell how life used to be before Christ*
2. *tell what God did for you*
3. *What God's done through you to help others*

God did it, not us changing His grace, mercy, forgiveness

minister out of our pain

11

4. What are some things people can share if they have been in the church all of their lives and were *not* saved out of a life of rebellion?

5. Why should you, when you tell your spiritual story, avoid making it look like positive changes in your life were the result of your own merit?

Learning from the Story

♘ In
horseshoe
groups of 6–8,
choose an
answer and
explain why
you chose
what you did.

1. What impression do you get of Paul from reading this story?
   ☐ He's an egotist.
   ☐ He "tells it like it is."
   ☐ He's not afraid of admitting his mistakes.
   ☐ He's too defensive.
   ☐ Other:_____

2. When and how did God "reveal his Son" to you?

3. What has God done in your life recently for which others might glorify Him?

write out spiritual story

② *write out your spiritual story*

③ *tell story by memory to 1 person*

ask a couple of mature Christians their story

①

life change lessons

1. Why does sharing your spiritual story require some advance preparation?

2. What kind of words should you avoid in sharing your spiritual story?

Caring Time

15-20 minutes

This is the time for developing and expressing your caring for each other. Thank God for the changes He has brought about in people's lives. Begin to pray for others who need Christ in their lives. Pray that we will have the courage to share our stories. Pray for these concerns and any others that are listed in the Prayer/Praise Report. Include prayer for the empty chair. Pray specifically for God to guide you to someone to invite next week.

Take turns praying, remembering the requests and concerns that have been shared. If you would like to pray silently, say "Amen" when you have finished your prayer, so the next person will know when to start.

Reference Notes

Use these notes to gain further understanding
of the text as you study on your own.

GALATIANS 1:11

brothers. Paul's word for fellow Christians. Even though he later has harsh words for the Galatians, they are still part of the same family of faith. His words come with the awareness of his relationship and are laced with love for them personally.

GALATIANS 1:12

revelation. Literally, "an opening up of what was previously hidden." Paul had certainly heard the "facts" of the gospel prior to his conversion, but he had violently rejected them as blasphemous. It was only after Jesus Christ revealed the truth and meaning of these facts to him on the Damascus Road that he accepted the gospel.

GALATIANS 1:13

my previous way of life. For other references to his previous way of life, see Acts 9:1–9 and 1 Timothy 1:13–16.

GALATIANS 1:14

traditions of my fathers. In particular, this refers to the oral law developed to explain and apply the teaching of the Old Testament.

GALATIANS 1:16

among the Gentiles. With Paul's conversion came his commission to preach to the Gentiles (Acts 9:15). In encountering Christ, he came to the realization that the Law was bankrupt (insofar as its ability to save anyone). Thus, there was no barrier preventing Gentiles from coming to Christ.

GALATIANS 1:17

Apparently the Judaizers (Christians who were arguing that Gentile converts had to obey the Jewish ceremonial law) had been saying that after his conversion Paul had gone to Jerusalem and there received instructions about the gospel. That would have meant he received it secondhand, and therefore his teaching had less authority than that of the other apostles.

apostles before I was. The only distinction Paul admits between his apostleship and that of the leaders in Jerusalem is that of time. They were commissioned by Jesus earlier than he.

Arabia. In the tradition of Old Testament prophets and of Jesus after his baptism, Paul retreats to the desert for solitude and reflection.

Jerusalem. It was a courageous act by Paul to return here—to his former friends who might well try to harm him because of his conversion to Christianity, and to Christians who might not even receive him because of their suspicions about him.

to get acquainted. It was important that Paul come to know the leaders of the church. They, in turn, needed to hear a first-hand account of his conversion.

James. James eventually became the leader of the Jerusalem church. He was a strict and orthodox Jew (see Mark 6:3; Acts 1:14).

Even though the Judaizers in Galatia might be critical of Paul, the Christians in Judea praised God because of him.

notes

Being Vulnerable

Prepare for the Session

	READINGS	REFLECTIVE QUESTIONS
Monday	2 Corinthians 12:6	Why do we judge people by what they "do or say"?
Tuesday	2 Corinthians 12:6	How often do your words match your actions?
Wednesday	2 Corinthians 12:7–8	What would keep you from being conceited?
Thursday	2 Corinthians 12:7–8	Think about why you struggle with pride as a human being.
Friday	2 Corinthians 12:9	When has God's grace been sufficient for you?
Saturday	2 Corinthians 12:9	How do you know when the power of God is resting on you?
Sunday	2 Corinthians 12:10	Have you ever sensed the truth of this verse in your life?

BIBLE STUDY

- to consider Paul's view of what it means to have weaknesses
- to learn to be honest about our weaknesses
- to understand that in sharing our weaknesses, we can help others deal with their weaknesses

LIFE CHANGE

- to learn what others see as our weaknesses
- to schedule a quiet time where we submit our weaknesses to God and pray that He will show His strength through them
- to share our weaknesses with a close friend or in a small group of believers this week

Icebreaker

10-15 minutes

GATHERING THE PEOPLE

◡ Form horseshoe groups of 6–8.

Secret Identities. Depending on the amount of time you have, you may want to choose two of the following three questions to discuss:

1. Introduce yourself to others in your group by filling in the blanks in this statement: "Disguised as a mild-mannered *(your occupation)*, my secret identity, known previously to no other mortal is *(your favorite childhood superhero)*."

2. If you could retain only one super power, which one would you keep (and why)?

   ☐ faster than a speeding bullet
   ☐ able to leap tall buildings
   ☐ more powerful than a locomotive
   ☐ become invisible
   ☐ super ESP
   ☐ fly over my enemies
   ☐ x-ray vision
   ☐ can shrink or grow at will
   ☐ immortal
   ☐ other: _____

3. If you had the super power of being in two places at once, where else would you like to be right now?

Information to Remember: In the spaces provided, take note of information you will need as part of this group in the weeks to come.

PEOPLE: Someone who is missing this week is:

What I can do to help this person know that he or she was missed is:

EVENTS: An event that is coming up that I want to make sure I am part of is _____. It will be _____ (time) on _____ (date) at _____ (location).

And if I have time, I would also like to be part of _____. It will be _____ (time) on _____ (date) at _____ (location).

Bible Study
30-45 minutes

The Scripture for this week:

LEARNING FROM THE BIBLE

2 CORINTHIANS 12:6–10

⁶Even if I should choose to boast, I would not be a fool, because I would be speaking the truth. But I refrain, so no one will think more of me than is warranted by what I do or say.

⁷To keep me from becoming conceited because of these surpassingly great revelations, there was given me a thorn in my flesh, a messenger of Satan, to torment me. ⁸Three times I pleaded with the Lord to take it away from me. ⁹But he said to me, "My grace is sufficient for you, for my power is made perfect in weakness." Therefore I will boast all the more gladly about my weaknesses, so that Christ's power may rest on me. ¹⁰That is why, for Christ's sake, I delight in weaknesses, in insults, in hardships, in persecutions, in difficulties. For when I am weak, then I am strong.

...about today's session

1. What mask does the leader urge you to remove?

2. What two reactions might people have if they don't see your need and vulnerability?

   _____

   _____

Identifying with the Story

1. Describe the attitude toward "boasting" in your home when you were a child by placing a mark on the following scale:

   ·

   1   2   3   4   5   6   7   8   9   10

   "Never toot your own horn!"   "If you've got it, flaunt it!"

2. Which of the following attitudes toward weakness or supposed weakness prevailed in your home when you were a child?

   ☐ big boys or girls don't cry
   ☐ admitting a weakness gives your enemies a chance to exploit it
   ☐ admitting a weakness is the first step in overcoming it
   ☐ sharing your feelings shows weakness
   ☐ other: _____

3. How do you feel about what Paul says here about weakness?

   ☐ confused—strength through weakness?
   ☐ irritated—He's just making excuses for himself!
   ☐ relieved—This means I can accept my weaknesses.
   ☐ other: _____

today's session

1. What were some of the things that Paul's enemies in Corinth criticized about him?

20

2. What message did God give to Paul about his weaknesses?

3. Who are some contemporary people that the leader referred to as examples of how God's power is made perfect in weakness? Can you think of others?

4. What two implications of what Paul says about weakness are there for your witness?

   _____

   _____

5. What problems are there with reasoning, "If people see my weaknesses, then they might not think I am a true Christian and it will hurt my witness"?

   1. _____

   2. _____

Learning from the Story

In horseshoe groups of 6–8, choose an answer and explain why you chose what you did.

1. What would be your closest equivalent to Paul's "thorn in the flesh"—a weakness (physical, emotional, or spiritual) that you have tried to get rid of but haven't been able to so far?

2. What would you say is the best way to deal with a personal weakness?

   ☐ hide it   ☐ work constantly at overcoming it
   ☐ be honest about it   ☐ submit it to the Lord
   ☐ other: _____

3. When has God shown His power by using you in spite of your weakness?

life change lessons

1. What are some ways you can learn about your weaknesses?

a. _____

b. _____

c. _____

2. Why is submitting your weaknesses to God a vital step?

Caring Time

15-20 minutes

CARING TIME

♘ Remain in horseshoe groups of 6–8.

Take time now to pray for one another and for your own special concerns. Remember the "thorns" that people mentioned ("Learning from the Story," question 1). Ask that God would speak to each group member about his or her weaknesses, as He did with Paul. Also, remember to pray about the concerns listed on the Prayer/Praise Report.

Pray specifically for God to guide you to someone to invite next week to fill the empty chair.

Close by thanking God for bringing you together as a group and by asking Him to help each group member grow spiritually.

BIBLE STUDY NOTES

Reference Notes

Use these notes to gain further understanding of the text as you study on your own.

2 CORINTHIANS 12:6

speaking the truth. This may infer that Paul's opponents had fabricated tales of their visions.

think more of me than is warranted. Apostolic authority is seen, not by a person's mystical experiences, but in the way a person lives and by the message the person preaches.

To keep me from becoming conceited. In fact, so wonderful were the visions Paul had been having that Paul needed to be brought back to earth via a very troubling physical condition.

a thorn in my flesh. It is unknown what Paul means here. Two viable options are: (1) a chronic physical ailment; or (2) the continual opposition Paul encountered. Speculation in the area of physical ailments has focused on a vision problem Paul may have had (see Gal. 4:15), or maybe a problem with seizures. It is significant that Paul generally used someone to write his letters (see for instance Romans 16:22), and when he did write with his own hand he mentioned the "large letters" with which he wrote (see Gal. 6:11). Such a vision problem may have started with the blinding vision on the road to Damascus. The speculation around seizures is also related to that experience, reasoning that his vision problem may have been part of a seizure, but there is little else to support such a perspective.

messenger of Satan. Sickness was thought to be caused by Satan, but the false apostles in Corinth are also referred to as servants of Satan (2 Cor. 11:13–15).

torment me. Literally, "to continually torment me." Whatever the problem was, it was chronic, though not debilitating.

Three times. There are parallels between Paul's experience and that of Jesus in the Garden of Gethsemane. Like Jesus, Paul was not delivered from the hardship that faced him; rather, he received strength to remain faithful in the midst of suffering.

the Lord. This is the only explicit reference in the New Testament to prayer made directly to Christ rather than to God.

This sentence is the lens through which all of 2 Corinthians must be understood as it reflects the fundamental misunderstanding that both the false teachers and the Corinthians had about the gospel. They thought that the power of God meant that Christians should escape or avoid the experiences of weakness, vulnerability, suffering, and hardship that are common to life. Paul's emphasis throughout the letter has been that the power of God does not mean such trials are avoided, but that God empowers believers to love, to bring healing, to serve, and to be faithful in the midst of such times (see 2 Cor. 1:3–11). Thus, the Christian life follows the pattern of the cross in which the glory of God was revealed through the suffering of Jesus on behalf of the world.

when I am weak, then I am strong. In asserting that his weakness made it possible for God to show His strength in him, Paul aligned himself with a perspective also voiced in the Old Testament. Gideon was told to make his army *smaller* so that people would not think their natural strength brought them the victory and would give glory to God in *His* strength (see Judg. 7).

notes

Becoming an Authentic Christian

Prepare for the Session

	READINGS	REFLECTIVE QUESTIONS
Monday	Acts 5:1–2	What part of your life do you keep back from God?
Tuesday	Acts 5:3–4	How do you handle confrontation?
Wednesday	Acts 5:5–6	When have you experienced a godly fear?
Thursday	Acts 5:7–9	When have you feared men over God? Why?
Friday	Acts 5:10–11	What event has God used to get your attention?
Saturday	Acts 5:10	How important is it for you to be an authentic Christian?
Sunday	Acts 5:11	How would you respond to those struggling with hypocrisy in your church?

BIBLE STUDY

- to learn what the story of Ananias and Sapphira has to say about being an authentic Christian
- to discover the qualities of an authentic Christian
- to look specifically at how to avoid hypocrisy in our Christian lives

LIFE CHANGE

- to find a spiritual advisor
- to read Scripture daily, remembering to apply it to ourselves
- to encourage Christian friends to give us both supportive and developmental feedback

Icebreaker
10-15 minutes

Caught Red-Handed. Have each person answer both questions before going on to the next person.

1. In which of the following areas of behavior did your parents catch you red-handed when you were a child or adolescent?

   ☐ skipping school
   ☐ smoking
   ☐ playing doctor
   ☐ looking at sexually-oriented material
   ☐ lying about where I was
   ☐ other:_____

2. What did your parents do and how did it affect you?

Information to Remember: In the spaces provided, take note of information you will need as part of this group in the weeks to come.

PEOPLE: A person here I don't yet know is:

Something I can do to get acquainted with this person is:

EVENTS: An event that is coming up that I want to make sure I am part of is _____. It will be _____ (time) on _____ (date) at _____ (location).

And if I have time, I would also like to be part of _____. It will be _____ (time) on _____ (date) at _____ (location).

Bible Study

30-45 minutes   **3**

The Scripture for this week:

¹*Now a man named Ananias, together with his wife Sapphira, also sold a piece of property. ²With his wife's full knowledge he kept back part of the money for himself, but brought the rest and put it at the apostles' feet.*

³*Then Peter said, "Ananias, how is it that Satan has so filled your heart that you have lied to the Holy Spirit and have kept for yourself some of the money you received for the land? ⁴Didn't it belong to you before it was sold? And after it was sold, wasn't the money at your disposal? What made you think of doing such a thing? You have not lied to men but to God."*

⁵*When Ananias heard this, he fell down and died. And great fear seized all who heard what had happened. ⁶Then the young men came forward, wrapped up his body, and carried him out and buried him.*

⁷*About three hours later his wife came in, not knowing what had happened. ⁸Peter asked her, "Tell me, is this the price you and Ananias got for the land?" "Yes," she said, "that is the price."*

⁹*Peter said to her, "How could you agree to test the Spirit of the Lord? Look! The feet of the men who buried your husband are at the door, and they will carry you out also."*

¹⁰*At that moment she fell down at his feet and died. Then the young men came in and, finding her dead, carried her out and buried her beside her husband. ¹¹Great fear seized the whole church and all who heard about these events.*

...about today's session

A WORD FROM THE LEADER

Write your answers here.

1. What examples of artificial things in our society are referred to in the presentation? What additional examples can you think of?

2. What examples can you think of where someone was an "artificial Christian"?

Identifying with the Story

In horseshoe groups of 6–8, explore questions as time allows.

1. When is the last time you remember being called on the carpet for something you did wrong or someone thought you did wrong?

2. How do you most often react when you are called on the carpet for something?

   ☐ I act guilty—whether I am or not.
   ☐ If I'm guilty, I can't hide it.
   ☐ I feel like a little kid.
   ☐ I get defensive, even if I'm wrong.
   ☐ I charm or talk my way out of it.
   ☐ I get angry and blow up.
   ☐ Other: _____

3. Had you been Ananias or Sapphira, and had you done what they did, what are the chances you would have tried the same cover-up and met the same fate?

   ☐ No way!
   ☐ A fair chance—I HAVE tried that approach before.
   ☐ A strong chance—I hate to admit when I have done something wrong.
   ☐ It's almost certain I would have been TOAST!

What is God teaching you from this story?

1. How was the Christian church using the proceeds of property that was sold and donated by members?

2. What examples are given of how hypocrisy has hurt the church in modern times?

3. What three approaches to dealing with hypocrisy are discussed?

   _____

   _____

   _____

4. What problems are presented by the "aim low" and "live and let live" approaches?

5. How does spiritual honesty help us avoid hypocrisy?

6. We should confront others with what they are doing wrong only after_____.

Learning from the Story

⊍ In horseshoe groups of 6–8, choose an answer and explain why you chose what you did.

1. How do you react emotionally to this story?

   ☐ shocked—that God and the disciples would have been so harsh.

   ☐ scared—maybe God would do the same to me!

   ☐ unsympathetic—Ananias and Sapphira had it coming!

   ☐ only somewhat sympathetic—it was a hard judgment, but a necessary one

   ☐ confused—I'm sure there was a reason for what happened, but I don't get it.

   ☐ other: _____

2. What do you think might have happened had God simply let this deception slide?

☐ Nobody would have known the difference.
☐ It would have encouraged more deception and hypocrisy in the church.
☐ It would have shown God's forgiving nature.
☐ It would have made people think that Christians were no different than anyone else.
☐ Other:_____

3. When have *you* felt tempted to make it appear that you were being more loving or sacrificial than you really were? What did you end up doing and how did you feel about it?

life change lessons

How can you apply this session to your life?

Write your answers here.

1. What Bible passage advises us to confess our sins to one another?

2. Why does confessing to another human reduce the temptation to be false?

Caring Time
15-20 minutes

CARING TIME

♆ **Remain in horseshoe groups of 6–8.**

Remember that this is the time for expressing your caring for each other and for supporting one another in prayer. Pray specifically that God will help each of you find a spiritual advisor and become more authentic in the way you live your Christian life. Also, pray for the concerns listed on the Prayer/Praise Report.

Continue to pray for God to guide you to someone to invite next week to fill the empty chair.

Close by taking a few minutes for each group member to say a brief prayer of thanksgiving for the blessings that God has graciously and lovingly given to him or her.

Reference Notes

Use these notes to gain further understanding
of the text as you study on your own.

ACTS 5:1–11

The hypocrisy of Ananias and Sapphira stands in stark contrast to the upbeat, positive picture of the early church presented so far. This action threatened the trust and integrity that formed the basis of the fellowship among the believers.

ACTS 5:2

he kept back. This rare Greek word is used in the Septuagint version of Joshua 7:1 to describe Achan's sin of taking part of the booty from Jericho that was to be devoted to God. Luke may be using this word to make a connection between Achan's sin and that of Ananias.

ACTS 5:4

You have not lied to men but to God. Peter's statement is not to minimize the fact that they *did* lie to people, but to highlight the fact that this lie was primarily an affront to God. Their lie showed that they failed to take the Holy Spirit's presence with the community seriously.

ACTS 5:5–10

Many today find this incident disturbing. However, it does need to be seen in light of the fact that trust was vital to this early Christian community. Those who were not true to their word threatened Christianity's witness. The surprise exposure of their sin and the direct act of God caused both Ananias and Sapphira to die.

ACTS 5:9

test the Spirit of the Lord. Their act betrayed their disbelief that God's Spirit really knew all that happened (Ex. 17:2; Deut. 6:16; Ps. 139:1–7). This verse shows how completely the early Christians identified God (v. 4) with the Spirit (v. 3) and with (the Lord) Jesus (v. 9).

ACTS 5:11

The result of this incident was that the entire community recognized the seriousness of the presence of God in their midst (Heb. 10:31; 12:28–29). *Great fear.* The early Christians were not afraid of being similarly struck down by God, but rather this should be more properly understood as, "they felt a great sense of awe at the power of God."

church. This is the first use of the word *ekklesia* in Acts. Although the English versions of the Old Testament do not reflect it, this word, along with *synagogue*, was commonly used in the Septuagint to translate the Hebrew word *qahal* referring to the assembly of God's people. Since *synagogue* became the name for the Jewish places of worship (the synagogue), the Christians used *ekklesia* to refer to themselves. By so doing, they claimed a common Old Testament term to identify themselves as the true Israel of God.

notes

Session

4

My Life as a Witness

Prepare for the Session

	READINGS	REFLECTIVE QUESTIONS
Monday	Matthew 5:13	Who influenced you to follow Christ?
Tuesday	Matthew 5:13	How is your life a preservative of the good news about Jesus?
Wednesday	Matthew 5:13	What in your life could hinder you from being an effective witness?
Thursday	Matthew 5:14	How does your life shine in your relationship with God?
Friday	Matthew 5:15	What causes you to be ashamed of the gospel?
Saturday	Matthew 5:16	How can you let your "light" shine?
Sunday	Matthew 5:16	Who would you like to bring with you to heaven?

OUR GOALS FOR THIS SESSION ARE:

BIBLE STUDY
- to consider what Jesus meant when He said we were to be the "salt of the earth" and the "light of the world"
- to understand why living our lives as witnesses, persons who tell others about Jesus, doesn't mean we have to be perfect
- to consider why what we do speaks louder than what we say

LIFE CHANGE
- to pray that you will live a Christlike life
- to list two or three behaviors you think are hurting your witness
- to get involved in one ministry where you can put love into action on a regular basis

Icebreaker

10-15 minutes

GATHERING THE PEOPLE

◡ Form horseshoe groups of 6–8.

(Carol)

The Light We Shine. What kind of light best describes each of the members in your group? For each of the lights below, choose a group member who best fits that category. Share these with each other in a spirit of affirmation.

CAMPFIRE LIGHT: You give warmth and light to a cold night.

FLASHLIGHT: You direct light to the especially dark areas where it is needed most.

100-WATT BULB: Your personality lights up the room!

FIREPLACE LIGHT: You bring people together around your crackling warmth.

MOONLIGHT: You reflect well the light of the Son.

SUNLIGHT: You are a natural light that gives life to those around you.

NEON LIGHT: Your light brings personality, flash, and color to the group.

Information to Remember: Finish the following sentences as you look around at the people here today.

1. A person in the group, besides the leader, I learned from this week was:

2. A person who lifted my spirits was:

Keep focus + Honor to God, not us!

Bible Study

30-45 minutes

The Scripture for this week:

LEARNING FROM THE BIBLE

MATTHEW 5:13–16

[13]*"You are the salt of the earth. But if the salt loses its saltiness, how can it be made salty again? It is no longer good for anything, except to be thrown out and trampled by men.*

[14]*"You are the light of the world. A city on a hill cannot be hidden.* [15]*Neither do people light a lamp and put it under a bowl. Instead they put it on its stand, and it gives light to everyone in the house.* [16]*In the same way, let your light shine before men, that they may see your good deeds and praise your Father in heaven."*

...about today's session

A WORD FROM THE LEADER

Write your answers here.

1. What are two attitudes people have while watching to see what Christians are doing?

   _____

   _____

2. What did the leader say is the essence of what it means to live for Jesus Christ?

Identifying with the Story

In horseshoe groups of 6–8, explore questions as time allows.

1. When it comes to flavoring the food you eat, are you more into:

   hot and spicy . . . . mild and subtle

   ketchup and   let the natural
   steak sauce . . . . flavors come through

   lots of salt and butter   air pop it and
   on popcorn · leave it plain

2. According to your natural personality, which are you more likely to do?

   . . . .
   1   2   3   4   5   6   7   8   9   10

   I shine my light from   I hide my light under a bowl,
   the hill for all to see!   and hope no one finds me!

3. If you could have a spotlight put on just one thing you have done in the past month, what would it be?

today's session

What is God teaching you from this story?

1. Why was salt so valuable in ancient times?

2. What are two inappropriate ways to react to Jesus' words that we are to be "salt" and "light" in the world?

   a. _____

   b. _____

3. How should a Christian deal with his or her imperfections?

   need to be a model —

God uses imperfect people—don't pretend to be perfect

4. If we truly want to be a light in the world, what light should we reflect? *the light of Jesus*

5. What two passages, both written by John, start with the phrase, "No one has ever seen God"? How is their meaning connected?

6. What would you say to someone who thought that to be "salt" and "light" in the world, a person has to be perfect?

4

Learning from the Story

In horseshoe groups of 6–8, choose an answer and explain why you chose what you did.

1. How do you feel about the idea of "letting your light shine" before people so they can "see your good deeds" and "praise God"?
   - ☐ It sounds like thinly veiled egotism.
   - ☐ It sounds scary—what if I fall on my face?
   - ☐ It's the kind of challenge I need.
   - ☐ If God helps me, perhaps I can do it.
   - ☐ Other: _____

2. Who, by the way he or she lived, shed light on *you* in your formative years?

3. In order to take this passage seriously, what is the first thing you need to do?
   - ☐ overcome my natural shyness
   - ☐ pray for God's strength for my weaknesses
   - ☐ free up some time to get involved in some caring ministries
   - ☐ conquer an enslaving habit that is making me a poor witness
   - ☐ other: _____

life change lessons

1. What needs to happen in your life for this session to be a success?

2. _____ is the _____ within you that makes the light shine forth.

Caring Time

15-20 minutes

Close by taking time to pray for one another and for your own special concerns. Thank God for the person(s) mentioned in question 2 of "Learning from the Story." Ask for strength to make whatever life changes people need in order to strengthen their witness. Also, use the Prayer/Praise Report and pray for the concerns listed.

Pray specifically for God to guide you to someone to invite next week to fill the empty chair.

Conclude your prayer time by reading Psalm 139:1–4,23–24 together:

> O Lord, you have searched me and you know me.
> You know when I sit and when I rise;
> you perceive my thoughts from afar.
> You discern my going out and my lying down;
> you are familiar with all my ways.
> Before a word is on my tongue
> you know it completely, O Lord.
>
> Search me, O God, and know my heart;
> test me and know my anxious thoughts.
> See if there is any offensive way in me,
> and lead me in the way everlasting.

Reference Notes

Use these notes to gain further understanding
of the text as you study on your own.

**MATTHEW
5:13**

salt. Salt was a very valuable commodity in ancient times. It was not only used to flavor foods, but it was indispensable in preserving them. In an age that had no freezers or refrigerators, salt kept food from spoiling. Salt solutions were used medically, specifically in washing newborn infants. Rock salt was also used as a fertilizer. Salt's value came from these many uses. Because of its value, Roman officers were given a salt allowance as part of their compensation. Our word *salary* is derived from that allowance, the *salarium*. When Jesus attested to the value of His disciples in the world, perhaps He had both salt's ability to flavor, as well as its ability to preserve in mind. Jesus' disciples are to flavor the world around them with God's love and direction; and they are to preserve that which is valuable in life from the spoilage caused by sin and hate. Christians who hold back from performing the function they are to have as salt are like salt that has lost its saltiness. In this passage, Jesus is probably alluding to rock salt, from which the salt could wash out. The resulting saltless white powder was used as a pavement for roads.

**MATTHEW
5:14**

light. Light is another basic element of life. The function of light is to illuminate the darkness. This is an image for the truth Christians are to bring to the world.

of the world. Israel was to be a light for the Gentiles (see Isa. 49:6). That function is now passed on to the followers of Jesus.

**MATTHEW
5:15–16**

The very purpose of light is defeated if it is hidden away. In the same way, Jesus' disciples are not to live secretly, but to live openly so that others can see who and what they are. The purpose of all this is not to focus on them, but to get people focused on God. Only if we give glory to God for what we do will this happen.

**MATTHEW
5:16**

let your light shine before men. What constitutes the "light" of Christians is what they say and do.

praise your Father. While persecution is the response that some people make toward those who embody the qualities of God's kingdom (Matt. 5:10), others will recognize in these qualities the character of God and give praise to Him.

notes

Spiritual Disciplines
in My Life

Prepare for the Session

	READINGS	REFLECTIVE QUESTIONS
Monday	1 Corinthians 9:24	What is the "prize" you are hoping to win in life?
Tuesday	1 Corinthians 9:24	What obstacles have you encountered along the racetrack of life?
Wednesday	1 Corinthians 9:25	Evaluate your spiritual life in light of this verse.
Thursday	1 Corinthians 9:25	What do you want to hear God say to you at the end of your life?
Friday	1 Corinthians 9:26	What is God's purpose for your life?
Saturday	1 Corinthians 9:27	What spiritual disciplines are a part of your life?
Sunday	1 Corinthians 9:27	What spiritual disciplines do you need to develop?

BIBLE STUDY
- to understand how disciplining ourselves spiritually is like how an athlete disciplines himself or herself
- to learn how to make spiritual discipline a part of our lives
- to talk about the importance of living a spiritually disciplined life

LIFE CHANGE
- to commit to a regular prayer time and a time set aside to be with God
- to set a goal for personal Bible reading
- to plan a spiritual life retreat

Icebreaker

10-15 minutes

Bring Out Your Best. Go around the group on the first question. Then go around on the next question.

1. Finish this sentence: "If you want to bring out my best, then ..."
   - ☐ feed me!
   - ☐ compliment my appearance
   - ☐ put me around playful people
   - ☐ give me a charge card and send me to the mall!
   - ☐ give me a challenge
   - ☐ give me lots of hugs
   - ☐ put me in a competitive situation
   - ☐ other: _____

2. Finish this sentence: "If you want to bring out my worst, then ..."
   - ☐ put me in a messy room
   - ☐ try telling me what to do
   - ☐ try putting me on a committee
   - ☐ give me a charge card and send me to the mall!
   - ☐ criticize me
   - ☐ make me eat health food
   - ☐ put me in a competitive situation
   - ☐ other: _____

Information to Remember: In the spaces provided, take note of information you will need as part of this group in the weeks to come.

PEOPLE: The person in the class with the biggest smile today is:

A person whose face has a look of concern and whom I should really talk with after class is:

EVENTS: An event that is coming up that I want to make sure I am part of is _____. It will be _____ (time) on _____ (date) at _____ (location).

And if I have time, I would also like to be part of _____. It will be _____ (time) on _____ (date) at _____ (location).

Bible Study

30-45 minutes

The Scripture for this week:

LEARNING FROM THE BIBLE

I CORINTHIANS 9:24–27

²⁴Do you not know that in a race all the runners run, but only one gets the prize? Run in such a way as to get the prize. ²⁵Everyone who competes in the games goes into strict training. They do it to get a crown that will not last; but we do it to get a crown that will last forever. ²⁶Therefore I do not run like a man running aimlessly; I do not fight like a man beating the air. ²⁷No, I beat my body and make it my slave so that after I have preached to others, I myself will not be disqualified for the prize.

...about today's session

A WORD FROM THE LEADER

1. What examples of discipline by athletes are referred to in this presentation?

Write your answers here.

2. What other examples can you think of?

5

Identifying with the Story

In horseshoe groups of 6–8, explore questions as time allows.

1. What did you do as a teen that required practice or discipline?

   ☐ playing a sport
   ☐ being in a play or musical
   ☐ getting my homework done
   ☐ playing a musical instrument
   ☐ dancing or cheerleading
   ☐ other: _____

2. How well did you discipline yourself for the activity in question 1?

   ☐ I was a real slacker.
   ☐ A parent had to remind me.
   ☐ I did it—*most* of the time.
   ☐ I was my own drill sergeant.

3. Finish this sentence: "The goal in my life that I have been most disciplined in trying to reach has been ... ."

today's session

What is God teaching you from this story?

1. Where else in Scripture did Paul use athletic imagery?

2. How should we apply Paul's reference to "only one gets the prize" to our spiritual lives?

3. What athlete can you think of who was once revered but is now booed or forgotten by others?

4. What does Paul mean when he speaks of beating his body?

5. What tools of spiritual discipline are referred to in this presentation?

_____

_____

_____

_____

_____

Learning from the Story

◡ In horseshoe groups of 6–8, choose an answer and explain why you chose what you did.

1. If an athlete disciplined himself or herself the way you do in your spiritual life, would he or she most likely be:

   ☐ a superstar
   ☐ a consistent winner
   ☐ one generally found in the middle of the pack
   ☐ a lifelong second-stringer
   ☐ cut in training camp
   ☐ laughed off the team

2. In order to strengthen your spiritual life, which of the following spiritual disciplines do you *most* need to work on?

   ☐ regular worship with the family of God
   ☐ maintaining a disciplined prayer life
   ☐ regular Bible and devotional reading
   ☐ making time for silence and solitude
   ☐ special disciplines like fasting and taking spiritual life retreats
   ☐ other: _____

**LEARNING
FROM THE
STORY
(cont'd)**

3. What help could you use from others in this group to do what you said you need to do in question 2?

- ☐ prayer
- ☐ suggestions on how to make time in my schedule for this discipline
- ☐ direction for Bible and devotional reading
- ☐ someone to check up on me and keep me honest—like my parent(s) used to!
- ☐ someone to pray with
- ☐ someone to go with me on a spiritual life retreat
- ☐ other: _____

life change lessons

**How can you
apply this
session to
your life?**

1. How can you remind yourself of planned quiet or devotional time?

**Write your
answers
here.**

2. Your choice of a Bible study goal would be:

Caring Time

15-20 minutes

**CARING
TIME**

**U Remain
in horseshoe
groups of 6–8.**

Remember that this time is for developing and expressing your caring for each other as group members by sharing any personal prayer requests and praying for each other's needs. Pray for the group member to your right that he or she will be able to follow through in the discipline he or she most wants to work on. Also, use the Prayer/Praise Report and pray for the concerns listed.

Pray specifically for God to guide you to someone to invite next week to fill the empty chair.

Reference Notes

Use these notes to gain further understanding
of the text as you study on your own.

**CORINTHIANS
9:24–27**

Paul turns to an athletic image to communicate the importance of self-discipline in the Christian life. This provides a transition to the call in chapter 10 to watch oneself and to forsake those things that would tempt one to fall away from Christ.

**CORINTHIANS
9:24**

only one gets the prize. Paul is not implying that in the spiritual life there is only one winner. All who put their faith in Christ and discipline themselves to do His will are winners. However, we should discipline ourselves *as if* there would be only one winner.

**CORINTHIANS
9:25**

crown. In the Greek games, the winner received a crown made of pine boughs. While simple and insignificant by today's standards, this crown conveyed a great deal of prestige. This prize was placed at the end of the race so that runners ran with their eyes on it. The Christian's prize is certainly more significant—eternal life with God. We must run our race, keeping our eyes on that prize.

**CORINTHIANS
9:26**

A runner in a race cannot simply run in any direction he or she chooses. The runner must stay on the course. Also, no boxer who swings wildly at the air will ever win, but rather those who concentrate on their opponent achieve victory.

**CORINTHIANS
9:27**

Paul applies the boxing imagery to himself as he wraps up his discussion of freedom in this chapter. Just as it is important for him to discipline his bodily urges (1 Cor. 6:12–17) so that he might be faithful to Christ's call, so, too, the Corinthians must exercise their Christian freedom in light of their responsibility to love. Otherwise, both he and they might be disqualified from God's race, like runners who left the track. Love, not "knowledge" (1 Cor. 8:1), is the essential demonstration of true faith.

5

notes

Caring for Others

Prepare for the Session

	READINGS	REFLECTIVE QUESTIONS
Monday	1 John 4:7–8	How are you doing at loving others?
Tuesday	1 John 4:9–10	Think about Christ's sacrifice for you—and fall in love with Him all over again.
Wednesday	1 John 4:11–12	How do you act toward your "dear friends"?
Thursday	1 John 4:13–16	How do you know that Christ lives in you?
Friday	1 John 4:17	Are you looking forward in confidence to meeting Christ on the Day of Judgment? Why or why not?
Saturday	1 John 4:18	What fears are you dealing with?
Sunday	1 John 4:19–21	Are there any Christian brothers or sisters you need to forgive—and love?

BIBLE STUDY
- to consider what it means to love one another as the Bible calls us to
- to understand that Jesus is the perfect example of how we are to love each other
- to think through the importance to our witness of caring for others

LIFE CHANGE
- to make a caring initiative this week toward someone we have had trouble with in the past
- to set aside at least one hour a week to give to people in need
- to find one way to act more lovingly to our families

Icebreaker

10-15 minutes

Old Friends. Friends are what make life good. They are also the ones who help you make it through when life is hard. Think back on some of your friendships.

1. Who did you consider your best friend (other than your spouse) during each of the following periods:

   ✧ childhood: _____
   ✧ adolescence: _____
   ✧ young adulthood: _____
   ✧ now: _____

2. Pick one of these friends and describe him or her to the group. How did he or she come through for you at a time when life was hard?

Information to Remember: In the spaces provided, take note of information you will need as part of this group in the weeks to come.

PEOPLE: A person here I don't yet know is:

Something I can do to get acquainted with this person is:

EVENTS: An event that is coming up that I want to make sure I am part of is _____. It will be _____ (time) on _____ (date) at _____ (location).

And if I have time, I would also like to be part of _____. It will be _____ (time) on _____ (date) at _____ (location).

Bible Study

30-45 minutes

The Scripture for this week:

[7]Dear friends, let us love one another, for love comes from God. Everyone who loves has been born of God and knows God. [8]Whoever does not love does not know God, because God is love. [9]This is how God showed his love among us: He sent his one and only Son into the world that we might live through him. [10]This is love: not that we loved God, but that he loved us and sent his Son as an atoning sacrifice for our sins. [11]Dear friends, since God so loved us, we also ought to love one another. [12]No one has ever seen God; but if we love one another, God lives in us and his love is made complete in us.

[13]We know that we live in him and he in us, because he has given us of his Spirit. [14]And we have seen and testify that the Father has sent his Son to be the Savior of the world. [15]If anyone acknowledges that Jesus is the Son of God, God lives in him and he in God. [16]And so we know and rely on the love God has for us.

God is love. Whoever lives in love lives in God, and God in him. [17]In this way, love is made complete among us so that we will have confidence on the day of judgment, because in this world we are like him. [18]There is no fear in love. But perfect love drives out fear, because fear has to do with punishment. The one who fears is not made perfect in love.

[19]We love because he first loved us. [20]If anyone says, "I love God," yet hates his brother, he is a liar. For anyone who does not love his brother, whom he has seen, cannot love God, whom he has not seen. [21]And he has given us this command: Whoever loves God must also love his brother.

...about today's session

1. What does the leader say people have a natural revulsion for?

2. According to this presentation, "To love people is to love _____."

Identifying with the Story

1. When you were a child, who defined love for you by the way he or she treated you and others? What one act can you remember that particularly illustrates this person's loving nature?

2. What has God done for you that has helped drive home the truth that "God is love"?

3. Which of the following phrases from this biblical text is most meaningful to you at this point in your life?

   ☐ "Whoever does not love does not know God, because God is love" (v. 8)—I'm tired of pious people who really don't care about me.

   ☐ "This is love: not that we loved God, but that he loved us and sent his Son" (v. 10)—This is the essence of the gospel.

   ☐ "No one has ever seen God; but if we love one another, God lives in us" (v. 12)—I got to know God through people who showed me His love.

   ☐ "There is no fear in love. But perfect love drives out fear" (v. 18)—God's love is more powerful than anything I fear!

   ☐ Other: _____

1. What is the difference in the meaning of the Greek words *eros* and *agape*?

2. What other Scriptures indicate a connection between loving God and loving people?

   _____

   _____

   _____

   _____

3. What are three things we can learn from how God loves us in Jesus Christ and how we are to love other people?

   _____

   _____

   _____

6

4. Name two other Bible passages that tell of how God showed the initiative in loving us.

   _____

   _____

5. What price did God pay to show His love for us?

Learning from the Story

⚘ In horseshoe groups of 6–8, choose an answer and explain why you chose what you did.

1. What qualities make it harder for you to love people as a "brother or sister whom you have seen"? How does this passage challenge you in relationship to such people?

2. What do you learn from how God expresses His love toward you, in relation to how He expects you to love other people?

3. If you were to take this passage seriously, what would be the first thing you would have to change about the way you relate to others?

life change lessons

How can you apply this session to your life?

Write your answers here.

1. To what does James compare those who hear the Word of God but don't act on it?

2. Three concrete ways you could put caring for others into action are:

   1. _____

   2. _____

   3. _____

PRAYER OF COMMITMENT

"Lord Jesus, I need you. I realize I'm a sinner, and I can't save myself. I need Your mercy. I believe that You are the Son of God, that You died on the cross for my sins and rose from the dead. I repent of my sins and put my faith in You as Savior and Lord. Take control of my life, and help me follow You in obedience. In Jesus' name. Amen."

Caring Time
15-20 minutes

Close by praying for one another. Pray for God's love to fill you in a new way and to help you take the "first step" you talked about in question 3 of "Learning from the Story." In addition, pray for the concerns on the Prayer/Praise Report.

Pray specifically for God to guide you to someone to invite next week to fill the empty chair.

Conclude your prayer time by reading together the words of Jesus in John 17:20–23:

> *My prayer is not for them alone. I pray also for those who will believe in me through their message, that all of them may be one, Father, just as you are in me and I am in you. May they also be in us so that the world may believe that you have sent me. I have given them the glory that you gave me, that they may be one as we are one: I in them and you in me. May they be brought to complete unity to let the world know that you sent me and have loved them even as you have loved me.*

Reference Notes

Use these notes to gain further understanding
of the text as you study on your own.

**1 JOHN
4:7**

love one another. John uses this phrase three times in five verses (see vv. 7,11,12). Each time, however, he uses it in a slightly different way. Here he urges his readers to love others because love originates in God. ***Everyone who loves.*** Since "love comes from God," all acts of love are reflections of God's nature in the believer.

**1 JOHN
4:8**

God is love. This is the second great assertion that John makes in this epistle about the nature of God. (His first assertion is that God is light.) This is one of the first truths we teach our children in Sunday school, and this is appropriate. To say that God is love is to say that love is at the core of God's nature, and so as children begin to know Him, this is a good place to start.

**1 JOHN
4:10**

Love is initiated by God. It is given substance by the incarnation of His Son. ***an atoning sacrifice for our sins.*** By this phrase John describes the saving work that Jesus did on behalf of the human race, thus opening up the way back to fellowship with God. The concept of atonement is seen in the Old Testament practice of substitution and sacrifice. In the Old Testament, sin was dealt with when a person symbolically placed his or her sins on an animal that was brought to the temple. This animal had to be perfect—without spot or blemish. It was then sacrificed in place of the sinful (imperfect) person. Such substitutionary sacrifices were a picture of what Jesus would one day do for all people on the cross.

**1 JOHN
4:11**

love one another. The second use of this phrase. The basis for this exhortation is the demonstrated fact that "God so loved us." Jesus' sacrificial death as atonement for sin on behalf of the human race shows people the depth of God's love and should thus release in them the ability to love others. Because they are loved, they can love.

**1 JOHN
4:12**

love one another. In the third use of this phrase, John states that although God cannot be seen directly, His love can be experienced as Christians love others. Since God is love, they know Him when they love.

**1 JOHN
4:13–16**

The Holy Spirit testifies to us that Jesus is God's Son. That's how we can know that when Jesus showed love, He was showing us something about the nature of God Himself.

1 JOHN 4:18

no fear in love. The reason for the confidence believers will have on the Day of Judgment is that they know God to be their loving Father (in whose love they have dwelt). To know you are loved by someone is to trust that he or she will never harm you and that you have nothing to fear in their presence. To know that God loves us is to know that we have nothing to fear because we know that God is more powerful than anything else in the universe. God's love trumps all of our enemies.

fear has to do with punishment. This is the heart of the relationship of people who approach God in fear: they think God is going to punish them. But if we are in Christ, then we need not fear punishment; rather, we rest assured of God's loving forgiveness.

1 JOHN 4:19

The love believers exhibit is a response to the prior love of God for them. Love begets love.

1 JOHN 4:20

Love for God is not merely warm, fuzzy feelings. Love is not love unless it finds concrete expression via active caring for others. Furthermore, since it is far easier to love a visible person than to love the invisible God, to claim success in the harder task while failing in the easier task is an absurd and hopeless contradiction.

6

1 JOHN 4:21

If people truly love God they will keep His commands, and His command is to love others. John reminds his readers of this one more time as he ends this session on love (see also 2:9–11; 3:10,23). To love God and to love others is a single, inseparable command.

notes

Learning to Affirm

Prepare for the Session

	READINGS	REFLECTIVE QUESTIONS
Monday	1 Thessalonians 1:2	Who do you thank God for consistently?
Tuesday	1 Thessalonians 1:3	What does your faith, love, and hope produce?
Wednesday	1 Thessalonians 1:4	Think about what it means to be chosen by God.
Thursday	1 Thessalonians 1:5	What sacrifices have you made for the sake of your witness among your friends and neighbors?
Friday	1 Thessalonians 1:6	Does knowing Christ as Savior fill your heart with joy? Why or why not?
Saturday	1 Thessalonians 1:7	How can you model Christ to other believers?
Sunday	1 Thessalonians 1:8–10	Is your faith known "everywhere"? Where is it known the most?

7

OUR GOALS
FOR THIS
SESSION
ARE:

BIBLE STUDY
- to take note of the consistency with which the apostle Paul affirmed the people in the churches to which he wrote
- to consider the effect of affirming other people on their work and witness
- to understand how a Christian community that practices affirmation can develop a stronger oneness with each other

LIFE CHANGE
- to write letters or emails of thanks to three different people within the next week
- to tell two different people at work what we appreciate about their work
- to affirm each suggestion that is made in the next meeting we attend

Icebreaker

10-15 minutes

GATHERING
THE PEOPLE

U Form
horseshoe
groups of 6–8.

Bullish on People. Over the past few weeks, we have "invested" in each other as a group. What kinds of investments have group members turned out to be? Look at the list and find a person in this group who best fits each category. Share these with each other in a spirit of affirmation.

BLUE CHIP STOCK: reliable one, performing steady and true

GROWTH STOCK: the one who has grown and "shot up" the most during these sessions

PASSBOOK SAVINGS: not flashy, but always available to the group

PRECIOUS METALS: showing his or her inherent (self) worth

COMMODITY FUTURES: one who shows a lot of potential for growth beyond this group

MUTUAL FUND: one with diverse strengths that contributed to the group

REAL ESTATE: where we invested a lot, but got a lot in return

RARE ART: one whose beauty as a person made it a pleasure to invest

Information to Remember: Finish the following sentences as you look around at the people here today.

1. A person here with whom I really need to talk is:

2. A person who looks like he or she could use some extra loving care is:

3. A person I wish I could get to know better is:

Bible Study

30-45 minutes

The Scripture for this week:

²We always thank God for all of you, mentioning you in our prayers. ³We continually remember before our God and Father your work produced by faith, your labor prompted by love, and your endurance inspired by hope in our Lord Jesus Christ.

⁴For we know, brothers loved by God, that he has chosen you, ⁵because our gospel came to you not simply with words, but also with power, with the Holy Spirit and with deep conviction. You know how we lived among you for your sake. ⁶You became imitators of us and of the Lord; in spite of severe suffering, you welcomed the message with the joy given by the Holy Spirit. ⁷And so you became a model to all the believers in Macedonia and Achaia. ⁸The Lord's message rang out from you not only in Macedonia and Achaia—your faith in God has become known everywhere. Therefore we do not need to say anything about it, ⁹for they themselves report what kind of reception you gave us. They tell how you turned to God from idols to serve the living and true God, ¹⁰and to wait for his Son from heaven, whom he raised from the dead—Jesus, who rescues us from the coming wrath.

A WORD FROM THE LEADER

Write your answers here.

1. What negative messages about yourself (like the one by Jonathan Edwards) do you remember hearing from pastors or church teachers in your spiritual journey? How did they affect you?

2. Do you agree that "people work best when they feel good about themselves"? Why or why not?

Identifying with the Story

In horseshoe groups of 6–8, explore questions as time allows.

1. Paul describes how the gospel, the good news about Jesus, came to the people of the church at Thessalonica. Which of the following sets of words or phrases best describes how the good news came to you?

gradually	in a flash of insight
with a quiet peace	with tears
at a time of great blessing in my life	during a time of great conflict in my life

2. The Thessalonians imitated the Christian example of Paul and his coworkers. In your Christian growth, who have you sought to imitate?

3. Who in your life has most affirmed you, as Paul here affirms the Thessalonians?

today's session

What is God teaching you from this story?

1. What spiritual leaders are mentioned as having used a positive and affirming approach to motivating people?

2. What did Jesus call Simon that affirmed him? What effect did this have on Simon?

3. Name two things Paul affirmed in the Thessalonians.

_____

_____

4. What did George Barna find out about affirmation in "turn-around churches"?

5. What two things does affirming others in the context of the church do?

_____

_____

Learning from the Story

In horseshoe groups of 6–8, choose an answer and explain why you chose what you did.

1. Who do you know who has recently become a Christian whom you could affirm for the enthusiasm he or she shows for the gospel?

2. Who do you know who, like the Thessalonians, serves as a model to other believers? Have you affirmed this person for his or her witness?

3. In terms of the ease with which you affirm other people, how would you rate yourself on the following scale?

. . . .

I'm a perfectionist—
my role is to tell people
what they could do better!

I'm an affirmer—
my role is to "catch
people doing right!"

7

life change lessons

1. We have a tendency to act like _____, or how people acted _____.

2. What attitude do you need to have toward yourself when you slip back into a more negative approach?

Caring Time
15-20 minutes

Take time now to care for one another through prayer. Go around the group and have each person pray for the person on his or her right. Thank God for that person and for the good things you have seen in his or her life. Also, use the Prayer/Praise Report and pray for the concerns listed. Start with this sentence:

"Dear God, I thank you for my friend _____."

Pray specifically for God to guide you to someone to invite next week to fill the empty chair.

Close by asking God to give each group member the strength and wisdom to accomplish the life change goals from this session.

Reference Notes

Use these notes to gain further understanding
of the text as you study on your own.

We always thank God for all of you. Paul usually began his letters with an affirmation of the recipients (see also Rom. 1:8; 1 Cor. 1:4; Eph. 1:15–16; Phil. 1:3; Col. 1:3; 2 Thess. 1:3).

faith … love … hope. Paul and other New Testament writers use these words (or a combination of two of them) as a way to sum up the essentials of the Christian life (see Rom. 5:1–5; 1 Cor. 13:13; Gal. 5:5–6; Eph. 4:2–5;

Col. 1:4–5; 1 Thess. 5:8; Heb. 6:10–12; 10:22–24; 1 Peter 1:21–22). Faith in Christ, rooted in the hope of eternal life, is expressed by love to others. These are active concepts, the presence of which is seen by tangible activities of sacrifice and service. It is not that these activities earn God's favor, but that their presence is proof of having received God's favor (see also 1 Thess. 3:6; 4:9; 5:8).

brothers loved by God. To pagans used to remote and unpredictable gods, this is a reminder of the intimacy with which God the Father relates to His people. Sharing in this common love is what makes the Gentile Thessalonians and the Jewish Paul brothers and sisters in God's family.

he has chosen you. Paul's purpose in reminding them of God's initiative in their salvation is to strengthen their hope in light of the pressures of external persecution (2:14) and internal uncertainty (4:13).

our gospel came to you ... with power, with the Holy Spirit and with deep conviction. See Acts 17:1–9. The success of Paul's mission is seen in his commendation of the Thessalonians (vv. 2–3; 4:1,9) and by the reaction of his opponents who resorted to mob violence to stop his work (Acts 17:5).

You became imitators of us and of the Lord. Discipleship means to become like one's teacher. Paul called people to imitate Christ (Eph. 5:1–2) and himself as a follower of Christ (1 Cor. 4:16; 11:1; Gal. 4:12; Phil. 3:17). In doing so, he echoed Jesus' call to " 'follow me' " (Mark 1:17; 8:34). The specific action commended here is their obedience to the gospel in spite of the opposition it created.

Macedonia and Achaia. These are the northern and southern provinces that made up Greece. Thessalonica was in Macedonia.

The Lord's message rang out from you. The story of their response to the gospel in the midst of conflict had spread throughout the area. Their location on a major Roman trade route and the intensity of the reaction to the gospel in their city easily accounts for the wide dispersion of their story.

turned to God from idols. This illustrates repentance, a decisive rejection of one's past lifestyle and false beliefs to embrace a new way (see Acts 3:19; 9:35; 11:21; 2 Cor. 3:16).

to wait for his Son from heaven. Uncertainty about the meaning and timing of the return of Christ led to the confusion this letter addresses.

the coming wrath. Both Jews and Christians foresaw a time when God would judge the earth. The gospel is the announcement that through faith in Christ believers are rescued from that judgment (John 3:36).

notes

Being an Encourager

Prepare for the Session

	READINGS	REFLECTIVE QUESTIONS
Monday	2 Timothy 1:6	How can you "fan into flame" the gift of God in you?
Tuesday	2 Timothy 1:7	When have you let a "spirit of timidity" creep into your life?
Wednesday	2 Timothy 1:8–12	In what circumstances have you been ashamed to be seen with other Christians?
Thursday	2 Timothy 1:13–14	How much do you depend upon the Holy Spirit to help you understand the Bible?
Friday	2 Timothy 1:15	Are there any circumstances in which you would deny Christ?
Saturday	2 Timothy 1:16–18	What believer have you "refreshed" this week?
Sunday	2 Timothy 2:1–3	What hardship have you endured as a "good soldier of Christ Jesus"?

8

BIBLE STUDY

- to learn how Paul encouraged young Timothy in the expression of his faith
- to better understand the importance of mutual encouragement in the church
- to recognize the most effective ways to encourage each other

LIFE CHANGE

- to tell each person in our families of one quality we see in him or her that gives us hope for that person's future
- to pause long enough to choose a positive reaction when people tell us their plans or dreams
- to find one person each week who is discouraged and give him or her a call

Icebreaker

10-15 minutes

GATHERING THE PEOPLE

◡ Form horseshoe groups of 6–8.

Don't Rain on My Parade! What if your friends gave a parade in your honor? What would it be like? Fill in the following to let us know how to set it up for you.

All of the floats would be made out of:

- ☐ roses
- ☐ orchids
- ☐ gold
- ☐ mountain wildflowers
- ☐ chocolate
- ☐ Legos
- ☐ other:_____

I would ride in:

- ☐ a Lexus
- ☐ a classic Corvette
- ☐ a Cadillac
- ☐ a giant pumpkin
- ☐ a fire truck (while clanging the bell!)
- ☐ a stretch limo
- ☐ an old Model T
- ☐ a horse-drawn carriage
- ☐ other:_____

The marching bands would all play:

- ☐ John Philip Sousa
- ☐ '60s and '70s rock
- ☐ John Williams sound tracks
- ☐ Country hits
- ☐ Jazz pieces

The only thing that could spoil it would be if:

☐ it rained all day
☐ my boss showed up
☐ they ran out of hot dogs and cold drinks
☐ other:_____

Information to Remember: Finish the following sentences as you look around at the people here today.

1. A person I want to hear more from today is:

2. A person God may be leading me to say something special to today is:

Bible Study

30-45 minutes

The Scripture for this week:

LEARNING FROM THE BIBLE

2 TIMOTHY 1:6–2:3

6For this reason I remind you to fan into flame the gift of God, which is in you through the laying on of my hands. 7For God did not give us a spirit of timidity, but a spirit of power, of love and of self-discipline.

8So do not be ashamed to testify about our Lord, or ashamed of me his prisoner. But join with me in suffering for the gospel, by the power of God, 9who has saved us and called us to a holy life—not because of anything we have done but because of his own purpose and grace. This grace was given us in Christ Jesus before the beginning of time, 10but it has now been revealed through the appearing of our Savior, Christ Jesus, who has destroyed death and has brought life and immortality to light through the gospel. 11And of this gospel I was appointed a herald and an apostle and a teacher. 12That is why I am suffering as I am. Yet I am not ashamed, because I know whom I have believed, and am convinced that he is able to guard what I have entrusted to him for that day.

13What you heard from me, keep as the pattern of sound teaching, with faith and love in Christ Jesus. 14Guard the good deposit that was entrusted to you—guard it with the help of the Holy Spirit who lives in us.

8

¹⁵You know that everyone in the province of Asia has deserted me, including Phygelus and Hermogenes.

¹⁶May the Lord show mercy to the household of Onesiphorus, because he often refreshed me and was not ashamed of my chains. ¹⁷On the contrary, when he was in Rome, he searched hard for me until he found me. ¹⁸May the Lord grant that he will find mercy from the Lord on that day! You know very well in how many ways he helped me in Ephesus.

¹You then, my son, be strong in the grace that is in Christ Jesus. ²And the things you have heard me say in the presence of many witnesses entrust to reliable men who will also be qualified to teach others. ³Endure hardship with us like a good soldier of Christ Jesus.

...about today's session

A WORD
FROM THE
LEADER

Write your
answers
here.

1. What discouraging sayings from our culture are referred to in the presentation? What others can you think of?

2. Name one encouraging Scripture you heard in today's session. What other encouraging Scriptures can you think of?

Identifying with the Story

♘ **In**
horseshoe
groups
of 6–8,
explore
questions as
time allows.

1. When did you receive a note or letter of encouragement just at the time you needed it?

2. Who is the "Onesiphorus" who has stood by you and encouraged you in a time of need?

3. Which of the things that Paul writes to Timothy do you most need to encourage you in your journey at this point in time?

- ☐ *"Fan into flame the gift of God, which is in you"* (1:6)—I need to be reminded that God has given me gifts I can use.
- ☐ *"For God did not give us a spirit of timidity, but a spirit of power"* (1:7)—I need to know that when I feel timid, God is with me.
- ☐ *"This grace was given us in Christ Jesus before the beginning of time"* (1:9)—I need to know I am part of something bigger than myself, something eternal.
- ☐ *"Endure hardship with us like a good soldier of Christ Jesus."* (2:3)—I need to know that when I suffer, I don't suffer alone.
- ☐ Other: _____

today's session

What is God teaching you from this story?

1. What professions are mentioned as particularly needing skills of encouragement?

_____

_____

_____

2. What two kinds of encouragement are needed by Christians?

1. _____

2. _____

3. What was the most intimidating challenge faced by the first-century church?

4. What two kinds of resources do we have to face challenges as Christians?

_____

_____

8

5. As Paul told Timothy, God has given us a spirit of
_____, of _____, and of _____.

6. One person who encouraged Paul and serves as an example to
us was _____.

Learning from the Story

⚘ **In
horseshoe
groups of 6–8,
choose an
answer and
explain why
you chose
what you did.**

1. Other than yourself, who do you know who needs the kind of
encouragement Paul gave Timothy? (Put names in at least two
of the blanks.)

   ☐ *"Fan into flame the gift of God, which is in you"*—Someone
   who needs to believe in himself or herself.
   _____

   ☐ *"For God did not give us a spirit of timidity, but a spirit of
   power"*—Someone who needs to believe God can overcome
   his or her fears. _____

   ☐ *"This grace was given us in Christ Jesus before the beginning
   of time"*—Someone who needs to feel he or she is part of
   something eternal. _____

   ☐ *"Endure hardship with us like a good soldier of Christ."*—
   Someone who is going through hardship and needs to see
   some purpose in it. _____

2. Which of the following actions do you think have the greatest
potential for encouraging other Christians?

   ☐ calling them on the phone to see how things are going
   ☐ sending them notes or emails that include uplifting
   Scriptures or stories
   ☐ sharing inspirational books I have read
   ☐ sharing tapes of sermons or Christian motivational speakers
   ☐ letting them know I am praying for them
   ☐ celebrating their successes
   ☐ other: _____

3. When it comes to encouraging other Christians, which of the following weather phrases best describes you?

- ☐ I'm usually "the rain on their parade."
- ☐ Well, maybe at least a "light shower on their parade."
- ☐ I'm "the cloud on their horizon"—I point out what *could* go wrong soon.
- ☐ I'm like "a partly cloudy day"—for every positive, I also point out a negative.
- ☐ I'm the "sunshine on their shoulder"—I always try to brighten people's day.
- ☐ Other:_____

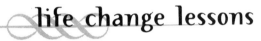

life change lessons

How can you apply this session to your life?

1. Why isn't accurately seeing where you are the only step you need to take to change?

Write your answers here.

2. If you have a tendency to be negative toward others' hopes and dreams, what is one step you can take to change that?

Caring Time
15-20 minutes

CARING TIME

♘ **Remain in horseshoe groups of 6–8.**

Take this time to encourage one another in prayer. Choose two people in your church who are involved in difficult ministries and pray for the challenges they face. Pray also for the concerns listed on the Prayer/Praise Report.

Pray specifically for God to guide you to someone to invite next week to fill the empty chair.

Conclude your prayer time by reading together some encouraging words from Paul in Philippians 4:6–8:

Do not be anxious about anything, but in everything, by prayer and petition, with thanksgiving, present your requests to God. And the peace of God, which transcends all understanding, will guard your hearts and your minds in Christ Jesus.

Finally, brothers, whatever is true, whatever is noble, whatever is right, whatever is pure, whatever is lovely, whatever is admirable—if anything is excellent or praiseworthy—think about such things.

BIBLE STUDY NOTES

Reference Notes

Use these notes to gain further understanding
of the text as you study on your own.

2 TIMOTHY 1:6

fan into flame. "Rekindle." Paul uses the image of a fire, not to suggest that the gift of ministry has gone out, but that it needs constant stirring so that it always burns brightly. He is also reminding Timothy of the power of the gift given him, as in the power of raging fire.

the gift of God. Paul reminds Timothy not only of his spiritual roots (the faith of his mother and grandmother), but also of the gift (*charisma* in Greek) he has been given for ministry.

2 TIMOTHY 1:7

Paul makes this sort of statement because Timothy is not a forceful person. *power … love … self-discipline.* The gift the Spirit gave Timothy leads not to timidity but to these positive characteristics.

2 TIMOTHY 1:8

ashamed to testify about our Lord. The gospel message about the dying Savior was not immediately popular in the first-century world. The Greeks laughed at the idea that the Messiah would die a criminal's death and that God was so weak that He would allow His own Son to die. And the Jews could not conceive of a Messiah (whom they knew to be all-powerful) dying on the cross (which they felt disqualified Him for acceptance by God). It was not easy to preach the gospel in the face of such scorn.

his prisoner. Paul may be in a Roman jail, but he knows that he is not a prisoner of Caesar. He is, and has long been, a willing prisoner of Jesus (see Eph. 3:1; 4:1; Philem. 1:9).

2 TIMOTHY **1:8** **(cont'd)**	***join with me.*** Rather than being ashamed of the gospel or of Paul and his suffering, Timothy ought to share in his suffering. ***suffering.*** Paul understands from his own experience and from that of Jesus that suffering is part of what it means to follow Christ (see 3:12; Rom. 8:17; 2 Cor. 4:7–15; Phil. 1:12,29; Col. 1:24; 1 Thess. 1:6; 2:14; 3:4).
2 TIMOTHY **1:9**	***has saved us.*** Timothy can face suffering because he has already experienced salvation. This is an accomplished fact. ***grace.*** God's work of salvation depends wholly on grace (His unmerited favor lavished on His creation) not on anything we have done. This grace, which was in place from the beginning of time, is given us in Christ Jesus (see Eph. 1:4).
2 TIMOTHY **1:10**	***appearing.*** The Greek word is *epiphaneia* (from which the English word "epiphany" is derived). It refers here to the manifestation of God's grace via the incarnation of Christ. ***Savior.*** This was a common title in the first century. It was applied to the Roman emperor (in his role as head of the state religion) and to various gods in the mystery religions. Christians came to see that Jesus was the one and only Savior. ***death ... life.*** Jesus' work of salvation is described in His twofold act of destroying the power of death over people (death no longer has the final word) and bringing resurrection life in its place.
2 TIMOTHY **1:12**	***I am not ashamed.*** That he is in prison brings no shame to Paul, despite how others might view it.
2 TIMOTHY **1:14**	***Guard the good deposit.*** In words paralleling verse 12 and 1 Timothy 6:20, Paul urges Timothy to preserve faithfully the "sound teaching" of the gospel.
2 TIMOTHY **1:15–17**	Paul now gives an example of those who have deserted him. To desert him implies deserting the gospel. Then, in contrast, Paul notes the extraordinary loyalty of Onesiphorus who went out of his way to search out where Paul was being held and then to "refresh" him.
2 TIMOTHY **1:15**	***Asia.*** This refers to what is now known as Asia Minor, but was then a Roman province with the capital at Ephesus.
2 TIMOTHY **2:1**	***grace.*** Grace is the sphere within which the Christian lives and moves. ***in Christ Jesus.*** The source of grace is union with Christ.
2 TIMOTHY **2:2**	Just as the gospel has been entrusted to Timothy (1:14; 1 Tim. 6:20), so he is to entrust it to others who, in turn, teach it to others. This whole process of entrusting is made doubly important by the fact that Paul will soon call Timothy to join him in Rome, implying that others will have to take over his ministry in Ephesus.

8

notes

Session

9

Ministering to One Another

Prepare for the Session

	READINGS	REFLECTIVE QUESTIONS
Monday	Matthew 25:31–33	How much are you looking forward to Christ coming back "in his glory"?
Tuesday	Matthew 25:34	What does having a place in the kingdom mean to you?
Wednesday	Matthew 25:35–36	What have you done to minister for Christ this week?
Thursday	Matthew 25:37–39	How often do you go out of your way to help someone else?
Friday	Matthew 25:40–43	Can you remember a time when you turned your back on someone in need?
Saturday	Matthew 25:44–46	Why is it important for you to do something for "the least" in our society?
Sunday	James 2:14–17	How can you tell if your faith is alive and well?

9

BIBLE STUDY

- to sensitize ourselves to the needs around us
- to learn to see ministering to people in need as a way of loving Christ
- to explore the best ways to minister to the needs of others

LIFE CHANGE

- to make out a time-use budget, similar to a financial budget, that includes time for caring ministries
- to visit with the pastor about what he sees as caring ministries particularly suited to us
- to review caring ministries that we have committed to in other sessions of this study

Icebreaker

10-15 minutes

**GATHERING
THE PEOPLE**

**U Form
horseshoe
groups of 6–8.**

No Man Is an Island. A famous poem declares, "No man is an island, apart to himself." While that is true, some of us have sought to live an island-like lifestyle by separating ourselves from others through many ways. Which of the following land formations or natural phenomena most resemble the way you have sought to live your life?

ISLAND—I am a loner who likes my private time.

MOUNTAIN—I see myself as seeking to rise above the mediocrity around me.

ISTHMUS—I am the one who joins others together.

OASIS—I seek to be an island of life and refreshment in a dry world.

GROVE OF TREES—I live best in community.

JUNGLE—Full of life but with my dark, scary side, too.

FLOWERY MEADOW—I am colorful and inviting.

BLACKBERRY PATCH—I have good fruit, but watch my thorny side!

Information to Remember: In the spaces provided, take note of information you will need as part of this group in the weeks to come.

PEOPLE: A person here I really need to talk to is:

A person here who looks like he or she could use some extra loving care is:

EVENTS: An event that is coming up that I want to make sure I am part of is _____. It will be _____ (time) on _____ (date) at _____ (location).

And if I have time, I would also like to be part of _____. It will be _____ (time) on _____ (date) at _____ (location).

Bible Study

30-45 minutes

The Scripture for this week:

LEARNING FROM THE BIBLE

MATTHEW 25:31–46

[31]*"When the Son of Man comes in his glory, and all the angels with him, he will sit on his throne in heavenly glory.* [32]*All the nations will be gathered before him, and he will separate the people one from another as a shepherd separates the sheep from the goats.* [33]*He will put the sheep on his right and the goats on his left.*

[34]*"Then the King will say to those on his right, 'Come, you who are blessed by my Father; take your inheritance, the kingdom prepared for you since the creation of the world.* [35]*For I was hungry and you gave me something to eat, I was thirsty and you gave me something to drink, I was a stranger and you invited me in,* [36]*I needed clothes and you clothed me, I was sick and you looked after me, I was in prison and you came to visit me.'*

[37]*"Then the righteous will answer him, 'Lord, when did we see you hungry and feed you, or thirsty and give you something to drink?* [38]*When did we see you a stranger and invite you in, or needing clothes and clothe you?* [39]*When did we see you sick or in prison and go to visit you?'*

9

⁴⁰"The King will reply, 'I tell you the truth, whatever you did for one of the least of these brothers of mine, you did for me.'

⁴¹"Then he will say to those on his left, 'Depart from me, you who are cursed, into the eternal fire prepared for the devil and his angels. ⁴²For I was hungry and you gave me nothing to eat, I was thirsty and you gave me nothing to drink, ⁴³I was a stranger and you did not invite me in, I needed clothes and you did not clothe me, I was sick and in prison and you did not look after me.'

⁴⁴"They also will answer, 'Lord, when did we see you hungry or thirsty or a stranger or needing clothes or sick or in prison, and did not help you?'

⁴⁵"He will reply, 'I tell you the truth, whatever you did not do for one of the least of these, you did not do for me.'

⁴⁶"Then they will go away to eternal punishment, but the righteous to eternal life."

...about today's session

**A WORD
FROM THE
LEADER**

**Write your
answers
here.**

1. What twofold obstacle do many people feel stands in the way of them ministering to others?

   1. _____

   2. _____

2. What two factors help us see the importance of ministering to others?

   _____

   _____

Identifying with the Story

**In
horseshoe
groups
of 6–8,
explore
questions as
time allows.**

1. When did someone visit you at a time that you particularly needed it? What about that visit do you remember most?

2. Which of the areas of need that Christ mentions have you been most likely to face yourself over the course of your lifetime?

- ☐ meeting my basic needs, like putting food on the table
- ☐ meeting my social needs, like finding friends when I felt like a stranger
- ☐ affording the clothes I needed
- ☐ affording the kind of clothes I really wanted
- ☐ health needs—I've had some crises
- ☐ "prison"—finding support when I had gotten myself into trouble

3. Finish this sentence: "A time I was in need and was disappointed that more people didn't respond was when ..."

today's session

What is God teaching you from this story?

1. According to the leader, the story of the sheep and goats was not meant to negate the truth of _____.

2. Which of the needs Jesus mentions can be found in every neighborhood, regardless of its socioeconomic status?

9

3. Do you agree that "every neighborhood is a needy neighborhood"? Why or why not?

4. What are two approaches to helping people in need?

1. _____

2. _____

5. What can you do for a homeless person on the street if you feel that giving money may not be helpful?

6. What is the most important gift we can give anyone?

Learning from the Story

1. In the family in which you grew up, which of the following phrases would have described the attitude toward people in need?

   ☐ "God helps those who help themselves."
   ☐ "Give a person a fish and he eats for a day; teach a person to fish and he eats for a lifetime."
   ☐ "If you're in need, it's probably your own fault."
   ☐ "There's always enough in our pot for one more guest."
   ☐ "It's the obligation of the privileged to share with the unfortunate."
   ☐ "It's more blessed to give than to receive."
   ☐ "There but for the grace of God go I."
   ☐ Other: _____

2. If you could put a percentage on it (as they do with chances of rain) what would you say is the likelihood you refused Christ in the form of a person in need in the past week?

   ☐ less than 10 percent
   ☐ 10–25 percent
   ☐ 26–50 percent
   ☐ 51–75 percent
   ☐ 76–90 percent
   ☐ over 90 percent
   ☐ 100 percent chance!

3. What do you need to open up to in order to better live out the teaching of this passage?

- ☐ open my eyes to the needs around me
- ☐ open my wallet a little more
- ☐ open my mind and stop being so judgmental
- ☐ open my schedule so I can spend more time visiting
- ☐ open up to more effective ways of helping than just doling out spare change
- ☐ other: _____

life change lessons

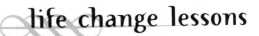

How can you apply this session to your life?

Write your answers here.

1. What kind of budget does the leader advise you to use?

2. What else can help you decide which caring ministry to get involved in?

Caring Time

15-20 minutes

9

CARING TIME

○ **Remain in horseshoe groups of 6–8.**

Use this time to pray for one another, remembering the needs expressed in question 3 under "Learning from the Story." Have each person in your group pray for one area of need in your community (homelessness, drug addiction, loneliness of the elderly, etc.). Also, use the Prayer/Praise Report and pray for the concerns listed.

Pray specifically for God to guide you to someone to invite next week to fill the empty chair.

Reference Notes

Use these notes to gain further understanding
of the text as you study on your own.

**MATTHEW
25:31**

he will sit on his throne. Because the Son of Man is sitting on His throne, the implication is that there will be a judgment.

**MATTHEW
25:32**

All the nations. This is a universal, worldwide judgment. While modern use of the word "nation" typically implies a political entity, here it refers to the various races and ethnic groups. All people will be present at this judgment scene.

separates the sheep from the goats. These animals grazed in common herds during the day. At night, however, they were separated because the goats needed to be in shelters to be protected from the elements.

**MATTHEW
25:34**

In this verse, the Son of Man (v. 31) is clearly identified as God's Son and the King of God's kingdom.

you who are blessed. The Beatitudes (Matt. 5:3–12) outline the qualities of those people who receive God's favor.

prepared for you since the creation of the world. Contrast this with the punishment of the wicked in the eternal fire "prepared for the devil and his angels" (v. 41). What God has intended and prepared for all people is the loving fellowship of His kingdom. People were not made for destruction although some choose it by rejecting Jesus as Savior. The place of eternal destruction was made for the devil and his angels. That the kingdom was prepared "since the creation of the world" for the righteous means that God's original intent was for people to share in His eternal kingdom of love and justice.

**MATTHEW
25:35**

I was a stranger. Hospitality to strangers was a highly regarded virtue in ancient Israel, possibly because it was a nomadic culture. The story of Lot and Sodom reinforced this virtue of hospitality to strangers (Gen. 19:1–26). The author of Hebrews may be alluding to this story when he says, "Do not forget to entertain strangers, for by so doing some people have entertained angels without knowing it" (Heb. 13:2).

**MATTHEW
25:36**

in prison. Probably those (like John the Baptist) who were in prison because they resisted the state out of faithfulness to God are in view. Visiting such a prisoner would put the visitor at risk since he or she might be identified as a sympathizer. It may also simply reflect the fact that many people were in prison because of their inability to pay off a debt. Hence, these too are the poor.

MATTHEW 25:37

Lord, when did we see you? The righteous did not act in this way because they had some type of insight regarding the spirit of Christ in the poor. They simply acted with compassion toward those in need.

MATTHEW 25:40

Just as Jesus served the poor and needy (both in a physical and spiritual sense), so He asserts that acts of mercy for the poor and needy are the way He is served in this world.

these brothers of mine. While it is uncertain whether this phrase actually is meant to reflect Christ's solidarity with all the poor or only with those who bear His name, such a debate may be akin to the question of the lawyer regarding just who was really his neighbor (Luke 10:29–37). The point is that the righteous are those who have a heart of compassion for all in need.

MATTHEW 25:41

The cursed are those who show a lack of concern for the needs of others.

the eternal fire. The idea of hell, a place of eternal punishment by fire, reflects Israel's experience with the valley of *Gehenna*, a ravine outside Jerusalem where children were once sacrificed to the god Molech (1 Kings 11:7). Jews considered it a defiled place, good only as a garbage dump that burned continually. *Gehenna* became a symbol for the place of punishment and spiritual death.

prepared for the devil and his angels. The Bible tells us that Satan led a rebellion of angels against God, and they were all condemned for it (see Isa. 14:11–15; 2 Peter 2:4; Rev. 19:20; 20:10).

MATTHEW 25:44

Lord, when did we see you? With this teaching Jesus condemned those who look past the suffering of the world as they seek a detached religiosity. The New Testament is consistent in saying that love of God and love of people, especially people in need, must go together (see Matt. 22:34–40; James 2:14–17; 1 John 2:9–11; 4:7–12,19–20).

9

MATTHEW 25:45

whatever you did not do. It is not enough simply to avoid doing bad things—people will be judged also for the good things they neglected to do. All can appeal to the grace of God in Jesus Christ, certainly, but the fact remains that God's expectation is that His children will do good as well as avoid doing bad.

notes

Building Relationships with Unchurched Friends

Prepare for the Session

	READINGS	REFLECTIVE QUESTIONS
Monday	John 4:4–9	What causes you to avoid someone? How can you treat others as Jesus did?
Tuesday	John 4:10–14	Have you drunk the living water Christ offers? How does your life reflect "a spring of water welling up to eternal life"?
Wednesday	John 4:15–18	How honest are you with God about your life—your sin?
Thursday	John 4:19–24	What helps you worship God in spirit and in truth?
Friday	John 4:25–29	Who have you told that Jesus is the Christ? What is your biggest obstacle in telling others about Christ?
Saturday	Luke 19:1–10	How do you feel about associating with unbelievers? What does Jesus' example teach you?
Sunday	Luke 7:36–50	How deeply do you love God? Take some time to thank Him for the great debt His Son paid for you.

10

BIBLE STUDY

- to learn how Jesus related to people who were not traditionally "religious"
- to understand the importance of developing friendships with those outside the church
- to know how to show caring for unchurched people

LIFE CHANGE

- to evaluate our present friendship patterns
- to focus on developing or strengthening a friendship with a person who doesn't attend church
- to ask an unchurched friend about what he or she believes or values

Icebreaker

10-15 minutes

My Holy Places. In biblical times, there were a variety of places that were considered "holy places." What places are the closest to being "holy places" for you—places that you feel at peace in your spirit or feel close to God?

- ☐ a special place I go in the mountains
- ☐ my favorite fishing hole
- ☐ Do golf courses count?
- ☐ at the home of some close friends where we have had many spiritual discussions far into the evening
- ☐ a place I go in the country
- ☐ a little roadside chapel
- ☐ the place where I was saved
- ☐ the sanctuary where I was married
- ☐ other: _____

Information to Remember: Finish the following sentences as you look around at the people here today.

PEOPLE: A person here (besides the leader) I learned from this week was:

A person who lifted my spirits was:

Bible Study

LEARNING FROM THE BIBLE

JOHN 4:4–29

The Scripture for this week:

⁴*He [Jesus] had to go through Samaria.* ⁵*So he came to a town in Samaria called Sychar, near the plot of ground Jacob had given to his son Joseph.* ⁶*Jacob's well was there, and Jesus, tired as he was from the journey, sat down by the well. It was about the sixth hour.*

⁷*When a Samaritan woman came to draw water, Jesus said to her, "Will you give me a drink?"* ⁸*(His disciples had gone into the town to buy food.)*

⁹*The Samaritan woman said to him, "You are a Jew and I am a Samaritan woman. How can you ask me for a drink?" (For Jews do not associate with Samaritans.)*

¹⁰*Jesus answered her, "If you knew the gift of God and who it is that asks you for a drink, you would have asked him and he would have given you living water."*

¹¹*"Sir," the woman said, "you have nothing to draw with and the well is deep. Where can you get this living water?* ¹²*Are you greater than our father Jacob, who gave us the well and drank from it himself, as did also his sons and his flocks and herds?"*

¹³*Jesus answered, "Everyone who drinks this water will be thirsty again,* ¹⁴*but whoever drinks the water I give him will never thirst. Indeed, the water I give him will become in him a spring of water welling up to eternal life."*

¹⁵*The woman said to him, "Sir, give me this water so that I won't get thirsty and have to keep coming here to draw water."*

¹⁶*He told her, "Go, call your husband and come back."*

¹⁷*"I have no husband," she replied. Jesus said to her, "You are right when you say you have no husband.* ¹⁸*The fact is, you have had five husbands, and the man you now have is not your husband. What you have just said is quite true."*

¹⁹*"Sir," the woman said, "I can see that you are a prophet.* ²⁰*Our fathers worshiped on this mountain, but you Jews claim that the place where we must worship is in Jerusalem."*

10

²¹Jesus declared, "Believe me, woman, a time is coming when you will worship the Father neither on this mountain nor in Jerusalem. ²²You Samaritans worship what you do not know; we worship what we do know, for salvation is from the Jews. ²³Yet a time is coming and has now come when the true worshipers will worship the Father in spirit and truth, for they are the kind of worshipers the Father seeks. ²⁴God is spirit, and his worshipers must worship in spirit and in truth."

²⁵The woman said, "I know that Messiah" (called Christ) "is coming. When he comes, he will explain everything to us."

²⁶Then Jesus declared, "I who speak to you am he."

²⁷Just then his disciples returned and were surprised to find him talking with a woman. But no one asked, "What do you want?" or "Why are you talking with her?"

²⁸Then, leaving her water jar, the woman went back to the town and said to the people, ²⁹"Come, see a man who told me everything I ever did. Could this be the Christ?"

...about today's session

A WORD
FROM THE
LEADER

Write your
answers
here.

1. What percentage of people in the United States claim to be in church on any given Sunday?

2. Where did Jesus most often meet with people? Who was He most likely to be with?

Identifying with the Story

1. Where was the most popular "watering hole" (the place where everyone gathered for refreshment and conversation) when you were a teenager?

2. What group were you not supposed to talk to or socialize with in your teen years?

- ☐ the druggies
- ☐ people of another race
- ☐ non-church kids
- ☐ kids who smoked
- ☐ those "on the other side of the track"
- ☐ none of these—we could speak with anyone!

3. What was it that you most "thirsted for" during your adolescence?

- ☐ attention from the opposite sex
- ☐ respect and recognition for my achievements
- ☐ truly intimate friendship
- ☐ my parent(s) attention
- ☐ a place to belong
- ☐ forgiveness
- ☐ love
- ☐ other: _____

today's session

What is God teaching you from this story?

1. Why did the Jews look down upon Samaritans?

2. What is the probable reason this woman came for water at noon?

10

3. What was probably "the best thing of all" that Jesus did in responding to this woman?

4. How did Jesus respond when the disciples returned and found Him talking to a Samaritan woman?

5. What three lessons do we learn from Jesus' interaction with this woman?

1. _____

2. _____

3. _____

Learning from the Story

1. If you were to encounter Jesus face-to-face, as this woman did, what one question would you most want to ask Him?

2. Of the things Jesus did in this encounter, which one would impress you the most had you been the woman at the well?

   ☐ just talking to me at all, when it wasn't socially acceptable
   ☐ not taking sides in the religious/cultural dispute over where one was to worship
   ☐ His knowledge of my past
   ☐ His acceptance of me in spite of my past

3. How do you react when someone finds you doing something that is not acceptable in your culture, as Jesus was by talking to a Samaritan woman?

   ☐ I try to justify my actions.
   ☐ I do what I think is right and don't worry about others' reactions.
   ☐ I'm careful to never do anything not approved of in my culture.
   ☐ I just pretend it didn't happen.
   ☐ I get angry at their narrow-mindedness.
   ☐ Other:_____

life change lessons

How can you
apply this
session to
your life?

Write your
answers
here.

1. For too many Christians, evangelism only happens in these two places:

   _____

   _____

2. What can you do in order to develop or strengthen a friendship with an unchurched person?

Caring Time

15-20 minutes

Close by sharing prayer requests and praying for one another. Have each person in your group share the name of an unchurched friend or acquaintance and something about that person. Then pray for the people named. In addition, pray for the concerns on the Prayer/Praise Report.

Pray specifically for God to guide you to someone to invite next week to fill the empty chair.

10

Reference Notes

Use these notes to gain further understanding
of the text as you study on your own.

**JOHN
4:4**

he had to go. Probably prompted by the suspicion His popularity aroused.
Samaria. A territory sandwiched between the Jewish provinces of Judea
and Galilee. Samaritans were a race of mixed Jewish and Gentile parentage.
In Jesus' day, strict Jews (who considered Samaritans religious half-breeds),
would go miles out of their way to avoid Samaria entirely by crossing the
Jordan River and traveling on its east side.

**JOHN
4:5**

the plot of ground. Genesis 48:22 tells of Jacob having given some land
to his son, Joseph.

**JOHN
4:7**

a Samaritan woman. Not only were Samaritans despised, women were
considered to be of much less value than men. A traditional rabbi would
not teach women. In addition to this lower status of women, we find that
this woman is living an immoral life.
came to draw water. Noontime, during the heat of the day, was not the
time women would normally perform this chore. This woman probably
came at this time to avoid meeting up with the "more respectable women."

**JOHN
4:9**

Jews do not associate. A "good Jew" would not use the same cup or
bucket such a person was using. Jesus' request shocks the woman. Her
response may well be mixed with more than a touch of sarcasm.

**JOHN
4:10**

living water. This was a common phrase meaning water that flowed from
a river or spring. Water like this had better quality than the standing water
of a well or pond. Jesus, however, is referring to spiritually "living water"—
water that refreshes the soul.

**JOHN
4:13–14**

will be thirsty again ... will never thirst. In contrast to physical water,
which quenches the thirst only for awhile, what Jesus gives will quench
the spiritual thirst of people, permanently filling their need. In Matthew
5:6 Jesus said, "Blessed are those who hunger and thirst for righteousness,
for they will be filled."

**JOHN
4:17–18**

While clearly revealing His knowledge of her situation, Jesus commends
her truthfulness. Women at this time could be divorced for trivial reasons
but had no right to divorce their husbands.

JOHN 4:20

mountain. This issue was a source of great hostility between Jews and Samaritans. Jewish zealots had destroyed the Samaritan temple at Mt. Gerizim many years before, and Samaritans had, at times, retaliated by desecrating the Jerusalem temple. See Deuteronomy 11:29 and Judges 9:7 as examples of worship on Mt. Gerizim. The woman may have been referring to this conflict to see whose "side" Jesus was on, and whether He would really speak to Samaritans.

JOHN 4:21

neither on this mountain. By this pronouncement Jesus refuses to take sides in a cultural argument. Rather, He seeks to point to the fact that it is the spirit with which one worships that matters.

JOHN 4:25

Messiah. The Samaritan's concept of the Messiah (based on Deut. 18:18) was less politically charged than that of the Jews. To the Samaritans, the Messiah was the One who would restore true worship and teach as Moses had done. Given this contrast, Jesus could affirm this title for Himself without fear of its being misinterpreted in political terms.

JOHN 4:27

talking with a woman. One rabbinical saying cautioned a rabbi against talking even with his wife in public on account of what others, not knowing she was his wife, might say. The concern was not just with the rabbi's reputation, but with the fact that women were thought unworthy to be taught God's Law.

10

notes

Sharing My Faith

Prepare for the Session

	READINGS	REFLECTIVE QUESTIONS
Monday	Acts 8:26	When have you felt the Holy Spirit guiding you in your life?
Tuesday	Acts 8:27–31	Do you understand the Bible well enough to explain it to someone who's interested in Christ? Why or why not?
Wednesday	Acts 8:32–35	To whom have you explained the good news of Jesus?
Thursday	Acts 8:36–40	When was the last time you went on your way rejoicing because of God's grace and forgiveness in your life?
Friday	Matthew 5:6	How much do you hunger and thirst for righteousness?
Saturday	Isaiah 53:1–7	Consider for a few moments the price that Christ paid for you.
Sunday	Matthew 13:1–23	What could you do to improve the spiritual soil of your life?

11

BIBLE STUDY
- to learn how Philip shared his faith with the Ethiopian eunuch
- to learn some effective methods used in the Bible for sharing faith
- to consider the Holy Spirit's role in our faith-sharing

LIFE CHANGE
- to pray daily for God to guide us to receptive people
- to pray for three or four days, then make a list of people we believe God is leading us to speak to
- to review our spiritual stories we wrote out in session 1
- to witness to at least one person this week

Icebreaker

10-15 minutes

This Week's Harvest. If you were to describe what you feel you have "harvested" or accomplished this past week, what kind of harvest would it be?

- ☐ back to "dust bowl" days—not a plant in sight has survived
- ☐ some shriveled fruit—enough to stave off starvation
- ☐ a below-average crop—nothing to be proud of
- ☐ an average crop—there are some successes I could point out
- ☐ an above-average crop—there are many successes I could point out
- ☐ a bumper crop—everything I touched thrived

Information to Remember: Finish the following sentences as you look around at the people here today.

PEOPLE: A person here (besides the leader) I learned from this week was:

A person who lifted my spirits was:

Bible Study

The Scripture for this week:

LEARNING FROM THE BIBLE

ACTS 8:26–40

²⁶An angel of the Lord said to Philip, "Go south to the road—the desert road—that goes down from Jerusalem to Gaza." ²⁷So he started out, and on his way he met an Ethiopian eunuch, an important official in charge of all the treasury of Candace, queen of the Ethiopians. This man had gone to Jerusalem to worship, ²⁸and on his way home was sitting in his chariot reading the book of Isaiah the prophet. ²⁹The Spirit told Philip, "Go to that chariot and stay near it."

³⁰Then Philip ran up to the chariot and heard the man reading Isaiah the prophet. "Do you understand what you are reading?" Philip asked.

³¹"How can I," he said, "unless someone explains it to me?" So he invited Philip to come up and sit with him.

³²The eunuch was reading this passage of Scripture:

> "He was led like a sheep to the slaughter,
> and as a lamb before the shearer is silent,
> so he did not open his mouth.
> ³³In his humiliation he was deprived of justice.
> Who can speak of his descendants?
> For his life was taken from the earth."

³⁴The eunuch asked Philip, "Tell me, please, who is the prophet talking about, himself or someone else?" ³⁵Then Philip began with that very passage of Scripture and told him the good news about Jesus.

³⁶As they traveled along the road, they came to some water and the eunuch said, "Look, here is water. Why shouldn't I be baptized?" ³⁸And he gave orders to stop the chariot. Then both Philip and the eunuch went down into the water and Philip baptized him. ³⁹When they came up out of the water, the Spirit of the Lord suddenly took Philip away, and the eunuch did not see him again, but went on his way rejoicing. ⁴⁰Philip, however, appeared at Azotus and traveled about, preaching the gospel in all the towns until he reached Caesarea.

11

...about today's session

A WORD FROM THE LEADER

Write your answers here.

1. What percentage of people did George Barna find believe strongly in sharing their faith, and what percentage did he find strongly believe they have no such responsibility?

2. What percentage of adults in the United States did George Barna find agreed with the statement that when another person tries to explain their religious beliefs, it is "usually annoying"?

Identifying with the Story

☂ **In horseshoe groups of 6–8, explore questions as time allows.**

1. Finish this sentence with one of the choices that follow: "A time in my life when, like the Ethiopian eunuch, I was really searching for spiritual answers was ..."

   ☐ in college, when truth seemed up for grabs
   ☐ when a loved one died
   ☐ when I reached the top rung on the ladder and realized it was empty
   ☐ when I left home for the first time and experienced the diversity of the world
   ☐ when I reached midlife and was re-evaluating what it was all about
   ☐ right now
   ☐ that has never happened to me

2. A person who, like Philip, came alongside me in my journey and provided some insights was:

3. Compare your own coming to Christ with the Ethiopian eunuch, by using the following scales:

. . . .

Like the eunuch, my coming   My coming to Christ
was an abrupt turnaround.   was gradual.

. . . .

Like the eunuch, a stranger   A close friend or loved one
gave me guidance.   "came alongside me."

. . . .

Like the eunuch, I was   God was searching
searching for God.   for me.

today's session

What is God teaching you from this story?

1. What aspect of this story of Philip and the eunuch is atypical of faith-sharing situations?

2. What were five important factors in Philip's faith-sharing?

_____

_____

_____

_____

_____

11

3. Why can it be a problem to witness indiscriminately to a person who is not ready? What saying of Jesus was this related to in the presentation?

4. What two ways of resisting the Spirit's leading are mentioned?

　_____

　_____

5. What else might a spiritually searching person be looking for, *other* than a way to heaven?

6. On what should faith-sharing focus if it is to be effective?

Learning from the Story

🐴 In
horseshoe
groups of 6–8,
choose an
answer and
explain why
you chose
what you did.

1. The most important factor in the success of Philip's witness to this Ethiopian was:

☐ God had prepared the eunuch to be receptive.
☐ Philip was obedient to the Spirit's leading.
☐ Philip knew the Scripture, so he could explain it.
☐ Philip responded to the questions the eunuch was asking.
☐ Philip's words were focused on what Jesus had done.
☐ Other: _____

2. In relationship to your own witnessing, rate yourself in the areas related to Philip's success:

I AM SENSITIVE TO WHO GOD HAS MADE READY:

. . . .

1	2	3	4	5	6	7	8	9	10

I generally haven't a clue.　　　　I almost always sense this.

I AM OBEDIENT TO THE HOLY SPIRIT'S LEADING:

. . . .

| 1 | 2 | 3 | 4 | 5 | 6 | 7 | 8 | 9 | 10 |

I often drag my heels.   I go where I'm led.

I KNOW MY SCRIPTURE AND CAN USE IT TO HELP OTHERS:

. . . .

| 1 | 2 | 3 | 4 | 5 | 6 | 7 | 8 | 9 | 10 |

Not at all.   A real strength.

I RESPOND TO THE PERSON'S QUESTIONS AND NEEDS INSTEAD OF ASSUMING I KNOW THE ANSWERS BEFORE HEARING THE QUESTIONS:

. . . .

| 1 | 2 | 3 | 4 | 5 | 6 | 7 | 8 | 9 | 10 |

Not true—   Generally true—
I follow my own agenda.   I first hear their need.

I FOCUS ON WHAT JESUS HAS DONE FOR US:

. . . .

| 1 | 2 | 3 | 4 | 5 | 6 | 7 | 8 | 9 | 10 |

Not really.   Always!

3. Finish this sentence: After evaluating myself in this way, the area I most need to work on in relationship to my witness is:

life change lessons

How can you apply this session to your life?

1. What four steps can we take to best prepare us to share our faith?

Write your answers here.

2. For what purpose might you want to review your spiritual story you prepared in session 1?

11

Caring Time
15-20 minutes

Go around the group and have each person pray for the person on his or her right. Pray especially for the person's greatest need in the area of witnessing that was expressed in question 3 of "Learning from the Story." Pray also for the Holy Spirit's guidance when witnessing. Remember to include prayers for the concerns listed on the Prayer/Praise Report.

Pray specifically for God to guide you to someone to invite next week to fill the empty chair.

Reference Notes

Use these notes to gain further understanding
of the text as you study on your own.

an angel of the Lord. Angel literally means "messenger."
the road. Two roads, one of which went through a desert area, led from Jerusalem to the old city of Gaza.

eunuch. Eunuchs were commonly employed as royal officials. Although he was attracted to Judaism, as a eunuch he would never be allowed to fully participate in the temple worship (Deut. 23:1).
Candace. A dynastic title for the Ethiopian queen.

chariot. While we have visions of light war chariots racing along behind fleet Arabian horses, it is probable that the eunuch was in a slow-moving, ox-drawn cart accompanied by a retinue of servants.

Do you understand what you are reading? This reflects how the apostles themselves could not understand the Old Testament prophecies about the Messiah until they were explained by Jesus after His resurrection.

The eunuch was reading from Isaiah 53:7–8, a key Old Testament passage about the servant of the Lord. This particular passage underlies much of what Luke has already recorded about the apostles' preaching concerning the identity of Jesus.

who is the prophet talking about ... ? The eunuch's question was a common one in Jewish circles. Some thought the prophet was speaking of

ACTS **8:34** **(cont'd)**	his own sufferings as one rejected while others thought he was speaking figuratively of Israel as a nation that suffered at the hands of its oppressors (Isa. 44:1–2). Most rabbis never attributed suffering to the Messiah. Neither had the rabbis made any connection between the suffering servant of Isaiah 53, the kingly Messiah of Isaiah 11, and the glorified Son of Man in Daniel 12. Only in Jesus' teachings did these truths come together (Luke 24:26).
ACTS **8:35**	Philip used this passage as a jumping off point to explain the ministry of Jesus. He undoubtedly referred the eunuch to other verses in Isaiah 53 as well as other references to the Servant in Isaiah which point out the Servant's suffering for the sake of others and how this Servant would be a light for the Gentiles. All of this would have been related to Jesus' ministry, death, and resurrection. **Philip began.** Literally, "opened up his mouth." The same word is used in Acts 10:34; it connotes a solemn pronouncement.
ACTS **8:36–38**	**Why shouldn't I ... ?** The Greek word behind this expression also occurs in the baptismal accounts of Cornelius in Acts 10:47 and 11:16-17. It may be part of a baptismal liturgy the early church used with candidates for baptism. The strict Jew would offer at least one reason why this man was ineligible to be considered part of God's people: he was a eunuch. Although due to his castration this man could never become a Jewish proselyte (see note on v. 27), he was able to become a full member of the church through Jesus Christ. This fulfills the prophecy of Isaiah 56:3–8 which anticipates a time when both foreigners and eunuchs would be welcomed into God's household. Luke may have included this particular event to illustrate just that truth.
ACTS **8:39**	**took Philip away.** Whether this was a miraculous act of God (1 Kings 18:12), or another way of describing a command of the Spirit to Philip (v. 26) is uncertain. **rejoicing.** The joy of the eunuch reflects that of the believers in Jerusalem (Acts 2:46) and Samaria (Acts 8:8), another evidence of the Spirit.
ACTS **8:40**	**Azotus.** Another city on the coast of the Mediterranean Sea, about 20 miles north of Gaza. **Caesarea.** The Roman seat of power in Judea, about 60 miles up the coast from Azotus. Philip evangelized throughout the Jewish communities along the Palestinian coast of the Mediterranean.

11

notes

Experiencing Authentic
Christian Community

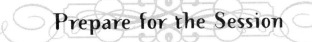

Prepare for the Session

	READINGS	REFLECTIVE QUESTIONS
Monday	Ephesians 4:11	What spiritual gift has God given you?
Tuesday	Ephesians 4:12	Who have you encouraged this week?
Wednesday	Ephesians 4:13	How mature in Christ are you?
Thursday	Ephesians 4:14	How easily are you swayed by any teacher?
Friday	Ephesians 4:15–16	Can others depend on you to speak the truth in love? Why or why not?
Saturday	Ephesians 4:25–28	How often do you "let the sun go down while you are still angry"?
Sunday	Ephesians 4:29–32	Which command listed in these verses do you most need to work on?

12

BIBLE STUDY

- to learn what made the Christian community of the early church strong
- to discover how a Christian community can deal with conflict in a healthy way to retain and strengthen the love in the community
- to understand what role emotional honesty plays in Christian community

LIFE CHANGE

- to affirm or encourage at least one person in each group we are part of this week
- to talk to a person in our church we need to forgive for a past offense
- to reveal one thing about ourselves that most people don't know (in the next session)

Icebreaker

10-15 minutes

All in the Family. In each of the following pairs, check which kind of person is most likely to get you "fired up":

The Bride of Frankenstein · Ken's Barbie
nobody mess with me!   in a fairy tale world

Lon Chaney, Jr.· Ken Griffey, Jr.
caught up in a   smooth as silk,
house of horrors   and on a roll!

George Bush, Jr. · Ted Kennedy
"compassionately conservative"   unabashedly liberal

Barbara Bush · Hilary Clinton
a supporter on the sidelines   charting my own course

Franklin Graham · Jane Fonda
following in a   always heading
parent's footsteps   in new directions

Information to Remember: Finish the following sentences as you look around at the people here today.

1. A person here I would really like to know better is:

2. A person in this group who has really been a blessing to me during these sessions is:

Bible Study

30-45 minutes

The Scripture for this week:

LEARNING FROM THE BIBLE

EPHESIANS 4:11–16, 25–32

11It was he who gave some to be apostles, some to be prophets, some to be evangelists, and some to be pastors and teachers, 12to prepare God's people for works of service, so that the body of Christ may be built up 13until we all reach unity in the faith and in the knowledge of the Son of God and become mature, attaining to the whole measure of the fullness of Christ.

14Then we will no longer be infants, tossed back and forth by the waves, and blown here and there by every wind of teaching and by the cunning and craftiness of men in their deceitful scheming. 15Instead, speaking the truth in love, we will in all things grow up into him who is the Head, that is, Christ. 16From him the whole body, joined and held together by every supporting ligament, grows and builds itself up in love, as each part does its work. ...

25Therefore each of you must put off falsehood and speak truthfully to his neighbor, for we are all members of one body. 26"In your anger do not sin": Do not let the sun go down while you are still angry, 27and do not give the devil a foothold. 28He who has been stealing must steal no longer, but must work, doing something useful with his own hands, that he may have something to share with those in need.

29Do not let any unwholesome talk come out of your mouths, but only what is helpful for building others up according to their needs, that it may benefit those who listen. 30And do not grieve the Holy Spirit of God, with whom you were sealed for the day of redemption. 31Get rid of all bitterness, rage and anger, brawling and slander, along with every form of malice. 32Be kind and compassionate to one another, forgiving each other, just as in Christ God forgave you.

12

...about today's session

A WORD FROM THE LEADER

Write your answers here.

1. What Christian writer and author is referred to as one who had to relearn what Christian community is about?

2. According to the leader, authentic Christian community is built around removing what from our lives?

Identifying with the Story

In horseshoe groups of 6–8, explore questions as time allows.

1. Which of the following phrases expresses the attitude toward anger in the home where you grew up?
   - ☐ "We don't get mad—we get even!"
   - ☐ "Don't ever let them know you're angry—grin and bear it!"
   - ☐ "Anger is dangerous—run and hide!"
   - ☐ "Get it off your chest—then kiss and make up!"
   - ☐ "Anger? What anger?"
   - ☐ "Anger is healthy, if communicated clearly and in a spirit of love."

2. In regard to how you are handling anger right now, how would you say you are doing in terms of verse 27?
   - ☐ The devil must feel he is on slippery sand!
   - ☐ The devil has found some footholds, but he hasn't gotten far "off the ground."
   - ☐ The devil has made it at least to base camp.
   - ☐ The devil is doing some high-altitude technical climbing!
   - ☐ By now he is posing for pictures on the summit!

3. How would you say your ability to handle anger has affected your ability to experience authentic Christian community?

☐ It's limited me to the superficial—as soon as there is conflict, I leave.

☐ It's destroyed some groups I've been in.

☐ We avoid anger in the groups I've been in.

☐ Working through conflict has been an important key to going to a higher level of intimacy in some groups I've been in.

☐ I don't see a connection between handling anger and experiencing Christian community.

☐ Other: _____

today's session

What is God teaching you from this story?

1. What is the "richer" meaning of the word *community*?

2. In a Christian community, what should we have in common?

3. What is the relationship of community to diversity?

4. How can spiritual immaturity hurt Christian community?

5. If we have God's love within us, what will we be strong enough to handle?

12

6. What are some unhealthy ways of handling anger?

Learning from the Story

In horseshoe groups of 6–8, choose an answer and explain why you chose what you did.

1. Which of the factors mentioned in this passage do you see as most important to establishing authentic Christian community? (Rank them from "1"—most important to "7"—least important.)

   _____ All are using their gifts for the common good (vv. 11–12,16).

   _____ There is an agreement on basic beliefs (v. 13).

   _____ People in the group are striving for spiritual maturity (v. 14).

   _____ People can speak honestly to each other (vv. 15,25).

   _____ Conflict and anger are handled in healthy ways (vv. 26–27).

   _____ People encourage each other and communication is positive (v. 29).

   _____ God's forgiveness is at the heart of the group (v. 32).

2. How would you rank *this group* on these factors? (Rank them from "1"—a real strength to "5"—a real weakness.)

   _____ All are using their gifts for the common good (vv. 11–12,16).

   _____ There is an agreement on basic beliefs (v. 13).

   _____ People in the group are striving for spiritual maturity (v. 14).

   _____ People can speak honestly to each other (vv. 15,25).

   _____ Conflict and anger are handled in healthy ways (vv. 26–27).

   _____ People encourage each other and communication is positive (v. 29).

   _____ God's forgiveness is at the heart of the group (v. 32).

3. In the spirit of verse 29, what is one word of affirmation you could give to build up the person on your right?

life change lessons

How can you apply this session to your life?

Write your answers here.

1. What groups will you be part of in the next week where you might practice encouragement and affirmation?

2. Who do you need to talk to in order to forgive them?

Caring Time

15-20 minutes

CARING TIME

Remain in horseshoe groups of 6–8.

During this time, thank God for the positive aspects of community that you have achieved in your group. Pray that God will work in your group to create honest, authentic community. Also, use the Prayer/Praise Report and pray for the concerns listed.

Pray specifically for God to guide you to someone to invite next week to fill the empty chair.

Reference Notes

BIBLE STUDY NOTES

Use these notes to gain further understanding
of the text as you study on your own.

EPHESIANS 4:11

This is one of several lists of gifts in Scripture (see also Rom. 12:6–8; 1 Cor. 12:8–10,28–30). No single list is exhaustive, defining all the gifts. Each is illustrative. The emphasis in this list is on teaching gifts.

apostles. Paul probably had in mind the small group of men who had seen the resurrected Christ and had been commissioned by Him to launch His church (see Acts 1:21–22; 1 Cor. 9:1). These would include the 12 disciples (1 Cor. 15:5) and a few others (e.g. Rom. 16:7).

REFERENCE
NOTES
(cont'd)

EPHESIANS
4:11
(cont'd)

prophets. In contrast to teachers who relied upon the Old Testament Scripture and the teaching of Jesus to instruct others, prophets offered words of instruction, exhortation, and admonition that were immediate and unpremeditated. Their source was direct revelation from God. These prophecies were often directed to specific situations. At times, however, their words related to the future (Acts 11:27–28).

evangelists. In the early centuries of the church, these were the men and women who moved from place to place, telling the gospel message to those who had not heard it and/or believed it. While all Christians are called upon to be witnesses of the gospel, the reference here is to those with the special gift of evangelism. This gift is the ability to make the gospel clear and convincing to many people.

pastors and teachers. The way in which this is expressed in Greek indicates that these two functions reside in one person. In a day when books were rare and expensive, it was the task of the pastor/teacher not only to look after the welfare of the flock (the title *pastor* literally means "shepherd") but to preserve the Christian tradition and instruct people in it.

prepare. These teaching gifts are to be used to train everyone in the church so that each Christian is capable of ministry. In other words, the prime task of the clergy is to train the laity to do ministry. In 3:12, Paul taught the concept of the "priesthood of all believers." Here he teaches "the ministry of all believers."

The aim of all these gifts is to produce maturity. Maturity is, in turn, vital to unity—the theme with which Paul began this section.

speaking the truth in love. Christians are to stand for both truth and love. Both are necessary. Truth without love becomes harsh. Love without truth becomes weak.

Therefore. This verse is a model for how Paul will discuss each of six topics. He begins with the negative deed, in this case, falsehood. (In Greek the word is literally "the lie.") Then he sets in contrast the positive virtue which he commends, in this case, truthful speech. Then he gives the reason for the command. Here the reason is that we are all neighbors. In fact, we are even closer than that, "we are all members of one body, the body of Christ." Lies destroy fellowship. Unity must be built on trust and trust comes via truth.

In your anger. Paul recognizes that there is such a thing as legitimate anger. Paul says in 5:6 that God experiences anger, though the translation obscures the meaning. (Although the phrase in 5:6 is rendered as "God's wrath," the same word there is here translated "anger.") Jesus was angry

(Mark 3:5). There are certain situations where anger is the only honest response. For Christians to deny their anger is dangerous and self-defeating. But once admitted, anger is to be dealt with, and so Paul gives four instructions on how to express anger. First, "in your anger do not sin." What is sinful is not being angry, but rather expressing it in a destructive way, by seeking to injure or destroy the person you are angry with. Second, "Do not let the sun go down on your anger," that is, deal with it quickly. Do not nurse anger and let it grow. Third, do not let anger develop into resentment. This is what the word translated "angry" at the end of verse 26 means. Get the anger out in the open. Be reconciled if possible. Apologize if it is appropriate. Fourth, "do not give the devil a foothold." Do not let Satan exploit your anger, turning it into hostility or using it to disrupt fellowship.

It is not enough simply to stop stealing; the thief must also start working.

From the use of one's hands, Paul turns to the use of one's mouth. The word translated "unwholesome" means "rotten" and is used to describe spoiled fruit (as in Matt. 12:33). Instead of rancid words that wound others, the words of Christians ought to edify ("building others up"), be appropriate ("according to their needs"), bring grace (this is the literal rendering of the word translated "benefit"), and not distress the Holy Spirit (by unholy words).

Paul identifies six negative expressions of anger which must be erased from the Christian life.

bitterness. Spiteful, long-standing resentment.

rage and anger. These two attitudes are related. The first is anger that is out of control in terms of how it is expressed, and the second is a more long-term, sullen hostility, where unexpressed anger has been allowed to grow in violation of what Paul said in verse 26.

brawling. Out-of-control, physical expression of anger.

slander. Anger expressed through verbal abuse.

malice. Wishing or plotting evil against another.

In contrast to the negative attitudes listed in verse 31, here Paul identifies a set of positive attitudes that ought to characterize the Christian. Instead of negative expressions of anger, the Christian ought to be kind, compassionate, and forgiving.

12

notes

13

A Legacy in God's Kingdom

Prepare for the Session

	READINGS	REFLECTIVE QUESTIONS
Monday	1 Corinthians 3:5	Do you see yourself as a servant? Why or why not?
Tuesday	1 Corinthians 3:6–8	What have you planted or watered for God?
Wednesday	1 Corinthians 3:9–11	Is your life built squarely on the foundation of Jesus Christ?
Thursday	1 Corinthians 3:12–13	What materials are you using to build your life?
Friday	1 Corinthians 3:14–15	What reward are you most looking forward to receiving from God?
Saturday	1 Corinthians 3:10–17	How can you promote unity among the Christians you know?
Sunday	John 4:27–42	What can you do this week to help bring in the "harvest"?

13

BIBLE STUDY

- to consider what kind of legacy we can have as Christians when we do God's work
- to learn what 1 Corinthians says about ways we can help build God's kingdom
- to review what we have learned in previous sessions and see how using our learning is important to our legacy

LIFE CHANGE

- to make a "will" that includes the spiritual qualities we would like to leave our families when we die
- to post a plan for "upgrading our building material" on our refrigerators or in some other visible place
- to periodically, such as once a month, write ourselves a "building progress evaluation"

Icebreaker

10-15 minutes

GATHERING THE PEOPLE

♘ Form horseshoe groups of 6–8.

My Small Group Is ... How would you describe your small group? Choose one of the images below that you think best describes your small group. Then go around your group and explain why you chose the one you did.

LITTER OF PUPPIES: We are a fun, friendly, and enthusiastic bundle of joy; I feel younger every time we are together.

SIX MUSKETEERS: It's "all for one and one for all" with this group; I always feel that I belong and that I'm part of a great team.

M*A*S*H UNIT: This group is like a field hospital; I came in wounded, and now I feel so much better—I have a bunch of friends to boot!

ORCHARD: Whenever I'm in this group, I feel like a fragrant, healthy apple tree because of all the growing I've done, and all the fruit I've been able to share.

OASIS: While the rest of the world can be so harsh and unforgiving, this group is a refreshing stop on the journey of life.

BIRD'S NEST: I know how a baby bird feels, because being part of this group makes me feel nurtured and protected.

TEEPEE: We couldn't stand tall and provide warmth and shelter if we didn't lean on each other.

Information to Remember: Finish the following sentences as you look around at the people here today.

1. A person in the class I would like to hear more from today is:

2. A person God may be leading me to say something special to today is:

Bible Study
30-45 minutes

The Scripture for this week:

LEARNING FROM THE BIBLE

CORINTHIANS 3:5–15

⁵What, after all, is Apollos? And what is Paul? Only servants, through whom you came to believe—as the Lord has assigned to each his task. ⁶I planted the seed, Apollos watered it, but God made it grow. ⁷So neither he who plants nor he who waters is anything, but only God, who makes things grow. ⁸The man who plants and the man who waters have one purpose, and each will be rewarded according to his own labor. ⁹For we are God's fellow workers; you are God's field, God's building.

¹⁰By the grace God has given me, I laid a foundation as an expert builder, and someone else is building on it. But each one should be careful how he builds. ¹¹For no one can lay any foundation other than the one already laid, which is Jesus Christ. ¹²If any man builds on this foundation using gold, silver, costly stones, wood, hay or straw, ¹³his work will be shown for what it is, because the Day will bring it to light. It will be revealed with fire, and the fire will test the quality of each man's work. ¹⁴If what he has built survives, he will receive his reward. ¹⁵If it is burned up, he will suffer loss; he himself will be saved, but only as one escaping through the flames.

13

...about today's session

A WORD FROM THE LEADER

Write your answers here.

1. What is one unsatisfying way of seeking a legacy that is referred to in the presentation?

2. A truly lasting legacy can be had only through contributing to what?

Identifying with the Story

⚲ In horseshoe groups of 6–8, explore questions as time allows.

1. Finish this sentence with one of the endings that follow it: "During my lifetime, I have spent the most time and effort building ... ."

   ☐ debt!
   ☐ my power base
   ☐ actual buildings
   ☐ faith
   ☐ frustration

   ☐ relationships
   ☐ memories
   ☐ my reputation
   ☐ family
   ☐ other:_____

2. What "Apollos" has been building alongside you, sometimes building on what you have done, and sometimes vice versa?

3. What have you achieved to this point in your life that you believe will have the greatest staying power—something that will last beyond a few years?

1. What message was Paul trying to get across to the factions in Corinth?

2. What example is given of a builder who lived a little before Paul and Apollos, whose building didn't last? Why didn't it last?

3. Who should our building be centered on if we want it to last?

4. Where did the churches that Paul and Apollos built worship?

5. If builders build without consulting the architect's design, what happens?

6. What is the significance of the reference in this passage to fire?

13

Learning from the Story

In horseshoe groups of 6–8, choose an answer and explain why you chose what you did.

1. As you evaluate what you have done to this point in your life, which of the materials that Paul mentions in this passage would you say you are "building with"?

   ☐ Gold—Much of what I'm doing will have a lasting, valuable impact for God.

   ☐ Silver—I can point to several things I have accomplished which will have a lasting, positive impact for God.

   ☐ Costly Stones—I haven't been a "world-changer," but I have had a positive, desirable impact on my little corner.

   ☐ Wood—I've worked mostly for common goals, just making it from day to day, but with a few more lasting accomplishments.

   ☐ Hay or Straw—I've never done anything that has meant much.

2. In order to "upgrade your building material," which of the following do you most need to do?

   ☐ work more at building people instead of building things

   ☐ work more at spiritual goals instead of just physical goals

   ☐ let Christ be my architect, directing how I build

   ☐ take time to evaluate my life, to be more intentional in the goals I am working toward

   ☐ other: _____

3. To strengthen your legacy, what do you most need to work on?

   ☐ being authentic and not hypocritical (session 3)

   ☐ using spiritual disciplines (session 5)

   ☐ caring for others (session 6)

   ☐ encouraging and affirming others (sessions 7 and 8)

   ☐ ministering to those in need (session 9)

   ☐ building relationships with unchurched friends (session 10)

   ☐ sharing my faith (session 11)

life change lessons

ow can you apply this session to your life?

Write your answers here.

1. What are some things people consider when making out their will? What are the implications of this planning for your spiritual legacy?

2. How often does the leader advise that you do a "building progress evaluation"?

PRAYER OF COMMITMENT

"Lord Jesus, I need you. I realize I'm a sinner, and I can't save myself. I need Your mercy. I believe that You are the Son of God, that You died on the cross for my sins and rose from the dead. I repent of my sins and put my faith in You as Savior and Lord. Take control of my life, and help me follow You in obedience. In Jesus' name. Amen."

Caring Time

15-20 minutes

CARING TIME

Remain horseshoe ups of 6–8.

Pray for the concerns listed on the Prayer/Praise Report, then continue with the evaluation and covenant.

1. Take some time to evaluate the life of your group by using the statements below. Read the first sentence out loud and ask everyone to explain where they would put a dot between the two extremes. When you are finished, go back and give your group an overall grade in the categories of Group Building, Bible Study, and Mission.

13

 GROUP BUILDING

On celebrating life and having fun together, we were more like a ...
wet blanket · hot tub

On becoming a caring community, we were more like a ...
prickly porcupine · cuddly teddy bear

 BIBLE STUDY

On sharing our spiritual stories, we were more like a ...
shallow pond · spring-fed lake

On digging into Scripture, we were more like a ...
slow-moving snail · voracious anteater

 MISSION

On inviting new people into our group, we were more like a ...
barbed-wire fence · wide-open door

On stretching our vision for mission, we were more like an ...
ostrich · eagle

2. What are some specific areas in which you have grown in this course?

☐ affirming and encouraging others
☐ using my life experiences to help others
☐ being mentored and/or mentoring an emerging leader
☐ developing a daily quiet time with God
☐ finding a way to use my gifts and talents in a ministry
☐ developing a habit of studying the truths of the Bible to help me with life change
☐ other: _____

A covenant is a promise made to another in the presence of God. Its purpose is to indicate your intention to make yourselves available to one another for the fulfillment of the purposes you share in common. If your group is going to continue, in a spirit of prayer work your way through the following sentences, trying to reach an agreement on each statement pertaining to your ongoing life together. Write out your covenant like a contract, stating your purpose, goals and the ground rules for your group.

1. The purpose of our group will be:

2. Our goals will be:

3. We will meet on _____ (day of week).

4. We will meet for _____weeks, after which we will decide if we wish to continue as a group.

5. We will meet from _____ to _____ and we will strive to start on time and end on time.

6. We will meet at _____ (place) or we will rotate from house to house.

13

7. We will agree to the following ground rules for our group (check):

☐ **PRIORITY:** While you are in this course of study, you give the group meetings priority.

☐ **PARTICIPATION:** Everyone is encouraged to participate and no one dominates.

☐ **RESPECT:** Everyone has the right to his or her own opinion, and all questions are encouraged and respected.

☐ **CONFIDENTIALITY:** Anything said in the meeting is never repeated outside the meeting.

☐ **LIFE CHANGE:** We will regularly assess our own life change goals and encourage one another in our pursuit of Christlikeness.

☐ **EMPTY CHAIR:** The group stays open to reaching new people at every meeting.

☐ **CARE AND SUPPORT:** Permission is given to call upon each other at any time, especially in times of crisis. The group will provide care for every member.

☐ **ACCOUNTABILITY:** We agree to let the members of the group hold us accountable to the commitments which each of us make in whatever loving ways we decide upon.

☐ **MISSION:** We will do everything in our power to start a new group.

☐ **MINISTRY:** The group will encourage one another to volunteer and serve in a ministry, and to support missions by giving financially and/or personally serving.

Group Directory

**PASS THIS DIRECTORY AROUND AND
HAVE YOUR GROUP MEMBERS FILL IN
THEIR NAMES AND PHONE NUMBERS.**

NAME

PHONE

Reference Notes

**CORINTHIANS
3:5**

servants. Paul and Apollos are not to be exalted. They are merely servants, and not of a very high order. They were simply carrying out the task God had called them to.

**CORINTHIANS
3:6**

I planted. Paul was the first evangelist to preach in Corinth.

Apollos watered. Apollos continued Paul's work by assisting in the building up of the new church.

God made it grow. Their labors alone would not have been enough. The divine life-force necessary to produce growth came from God (v. 7).

**CORINTHIANS
3:8**

one purpose. Paul and Apollos were colleagues, not rivals. They had the same ultimate purpose even though they had different specific tasks to fulfill. (One began the work; the other nurtured it.)

**CORINTHIANS
3:9**

God's field. The Corinthians are the field which God is plowing via His servants.

God's building. Paul shifts the metaphor from agriculture to architecture.

**CORINTHIANS
3:10**

I laid a foundation. By preaching Christ, who is the foundation (v. 11), Paul was the one who began the work in Corinth (v. 6).

expert. Literally, "wise." This reference is reminiscent of Christ's teaching about the wisdom of building on a rock rather than on a sand foundation (Matt. 7:24–25).

builder. This is one who plans and supervises the construction of a building, not the one who does the actual labor.

**CORINTHIANS
3:11**

A community might be built on another foundation (e.g., the leadership and ideas of a famous philosopher), but it would not be the church. The church's only foundation is the person of Jesus Christ (see 1 Cor. 1:18–25).

**CORINTHIANS
3:12**

Paul describes how a person can go astray (as he warns in v. 10) by using inferior or inadequate materials to build on the foundation.

gold, silver, costly stones. These materials will survive the test of fire.

wood, hay or straw. These will burn up.

**CORINTHIANS
3:13**

The Day. On the Day of judgment, the quality of such labor will be revealed.

fire. The idea is not of fire as punishment but as a means of testing, a way of revealing the quality of each person's work. This is a strong warning to those who lead the church.

**CORINTHIANS
3:15**

he himself will be saved. Here it becomes evident that Paul is not writing about what threatens salvation, but rather what threatens one's legacy, one's contribution to the kingdom.